CW00346833

Nelson Noonan

In Search of a Penguin's Egg

Nelson Norman

authorHOUSE®

AuthorHouse™ UK Ltd.
500 Avebury Boulevard
Central Milton Keynes, MK9 2BE
www.authorhouse.co.uk
Phone: 08001974150

First published by AuthorHouse 9/8/2009

ISBN: 978-1-4490-1729-3 (sc)

This book is printed on acid-free paper.

There is a tide in the affairs of men,
Which, taken at the flood, leads on to fortune
Shakespeare, *Julius Caesar*

This book is for my wife, Morag, with all my love and gratitude for her support through both good and bad times.

≈≥

Contents

Chapter 1

National Service

"Congratulations, you are 100 per cent fit," said the pompous chairman of the medical selection committee. I almost replied that I understood I would be deferred from National Service since I had had a minor gastric bleed when I was a student. I felt at a distinct disadvantage since I was standing naked before the group of venerable gentlemen with my bundle of clothes below my arm. So I just nodded and passed along the conveyor belt. I soon came to terms with the verdict, however, and was actually looking forward to the army when I was summoned to Edinburgh Castle for a second opinion. This time I was once again divested of my raiment and stood naked in the middle of a large chamber as two superior and slightly supercilious chaps slowly circumnavigated me and observed me in great detail. I was not a great physical specimen, but they gave me the impression that they were observing Michelangelo's statue of David. That thought was shattered when one whispered to the other, "Is he possibly just a tiny bit obese?" I was displeased because by that time, I was desperate to do National Service as a loyal subject of the crown. I told them so and was accepted.

National Service was a fantastic institution, and young people have lost much since it was discontinued. For me it provided a terrific adventure, which proved to be a central feature of my life. While I would love to have been an Army or Naval officer, I must admit that I was not cut out for such a role. I was already a qualified doctor when

I joined the RAMC, and I was clear on the direction which my life and career would take. I had considered this carefully as a schoolboy at Paisley Grammar School and as a medical undergraduate at Glasgow University. From an early age, all that would satisfy me was becoming a surgeon in Glasgow. If that was not possible, I had no idea what I would do. Since I had grown up during the Second World War, the travel restrictions in place had prevented me from venturing out of the west of Scotland before I went to university. My horizons were thus not very broad. This resulted in a rather parochial outlook, and it seemed to me then that the west of Scotland was the only possible place in the world to spend one's life. In retrospect, perhaps I was right!

By the time I had finished my house jobs at the Victoria Infirmary in Glasgow, National Service was in its terminal phase. I had always had a preference for the Navy since I loved boats, the sea, and the traditions of the Navy – possibly also because my name is Nelson. The Navy, however, required a commitment of four years, and since I did not want to be a grandfather by the time I was a surgeon, I joined the RAMC for the statutory two years. I was subsequently told that I could thank my lucky stars that I had not joined the Navy with a name like Nelson!

The dignity of the newly qualified doctor with a full year of worship by the nurses of the Victoria Infirmary was a bit dented by being loaded into the back of a truck at Aldershot station by a bunch of yelling NCOs. It reminded me of an often-seen picture of a shipment of inmates arriving at Auschwitz or Treblinka. We eventually arrived at the officers' mess at Crookham, and this was a very fine building, full of creature comforts. My spirits rose. It was, however, not for us. We soon found that we were to be housed in the grounds in little, very basic huts with tin roofs called "Spiders". They were heated by coal-burning stoves with iron chimney pipes protruding through the roof, and though we were four to a room, we did have a batman to polish our boots. He addressed one as "sir" – but he did not mean it! One night after a particularly jolly party, we were returning to our Spider when one of the Glasgow contingent climbed to the roof of the Spider in which the major commanding our intake lived and proceeded to pass water down the chimney. The major came rushing out in a great issue of sizzling sounds, steam, and a very bad temper. The poor chap had drunk so much beer that he could not stop and had to carry on through the shouting and screaming of the major. It did have to be one of us Glaswegians! I never did hear where the poor chap was eventually posted – possibly the bridge over the river Kwai.

We were drilled much, as you see in old movies, and it was quite good fun. The drill sergeants shouted and cursed us but ended each sentence with the word "gentlemen", and after calling individuals the most uncouth names, their diatribes ended with the word "sir". We were officers, you see. We had lectures on how to conduct ourselves as officers and gentlemen when with a regiment and courses on various aspects of army health, hygiene, and procedure. They told us that they would make every endeavour to post us to our preferred place. Many of my friends were to be married soon, and they asked for home postings. But being fancy free and looking for some adventure, I said I would go anywhere so long as it was far away because I wanted to see the world. The married chaps were nearly all sent to the Far East, Germany, or even to the Trucial Oman Scouts in one case! I was told that I was going to Northern Ireland. I was displeased. I felt like reminding them that I had not passed water down the CO's chimney.

A few days later, we were visited by a Mr Sloman from the Crown Agents who said he was looking for a doctor to serve on the Falkland Islands Dependencies Survey. Although I had been firmly advised never to volunteer for anything in the Army, I asked a colleague where the Falkland Islands were and whether he knew about this posting. He said at once that they were off the coast of South America, and he thought the job entailed joining a ship and touring around stations in South America to care for the personnel on isolated communities there. South America, I thought, sounded great, for I was secretly in love with Carmen Miranda and still yearned for boats and the sea. I quickly volunteered for the post without further thought or a request for more information since I wanted to be first in the queue. After all, it could hardly be worse than Ireland! That was the last I heard about it, and several weeks later, I assumed that I had not been selected. So I just settled down to my lot in Northern Ireland.

I have a great admiration for the Army. The Royal Warwickshire

Regiment, which was my posting, was a very fine regiment, but I was not cut out to be a soldier. I found it difficult to fit into the mould. Since my basic training had been interrupted by a requirement to attend the High Court in Glasgow as an expert witness in a case that I had treated in the casualty department there, I had missed so many lectures that the procedure in the Army was difficult for me, to say the least. The battalion was preparing to move for a tour in Aden, and that sounded interesting and exciting, so I phoned the ADMS in Lisburn to ask whether I would be accompanying it. The answer was, "No, because orders have come through for you to join the Falklands Islands Dependencies Survey, and you are to report to the Crown agents on Monday first. Leave in two days' time for the Headquarters Mess in Millbank." That was a bit of a shock, but I suppose, all things considered, it was for the best.

Before I left Ireland, the battalion dined me out. It was a truly wonderful occasion with a waiter behind each chair, a huge heap of regimental silver on the table, and the band playing in the background. This time I had rehearsed and got nearly everything right – I even made it in and out of the dining room in the correct order! The only gaff was that I ate the colonel's peach. The picture of that wonderful occasion will live with me forever and make me proud of my short association with that great regiment.

Chapter 2

Who said anything about the Antarctic?

When I arrived in London I was installed in the magnificent RAMC Headquarters Mess at Millbank, complete with a real batman, and on Monday morning I found myself sitting across the table from a delightful and venerable old gentleman whose assistant, Ann Todd, introduced as Sir Raymond Priestley. His first words were, "Tell me, my boy, why do you want to go to the Antarctic?" I have no idea now how I replied, but my thought was, "Who said anything about the Antarctic? I want to go to South America." They must have been pretty desperate to find a doctor because my total fund of Antarctic knowledge was that I had heard of Scott, Shackleton, and Amundsen! Yet that was how an adventure which coloured the course of my whole life started. If I had had a little more general knowledge, I would have known that Sir Raymond was a member of Captain Scott's last expedition and that the Falkland Islands Dependencies were British Antarctic Territories! Sir Raymond told me that I was going to Halley Bay on the coast of the Weddell Sea and that it was the most southerly British base, being about 800 miles from the South Pole. The base had been established by the Royal Society as its contribution to the International Geophysical Year (IGY), but it was being taken over by the Falkland Islands Dependencies Survey – known as FIDS – as a geophysical observatory. When I told my sister Margaret in Cheltenham that I was going to the Antarctic her response was, "But you do not even like a draught." Yet I was delighted that I had almost accidentally stumbled into an Antarctic expedition, and the more I thought about it, the more excited I became about the challenge and the prospect.

I then met Bill Sloman again, and he confirmed that I would be going to Halley Bay, on the Brunt Ice Shelf in the Weddell Sea, but he assured me that I would only have to pay Falkland Islands income tax. Since the pay was £640 per year, it seemed to me that the standard of tax was immaterial. He also told me that I would have the medical kit of a battle cruiser to care for ten men and that he thought that ought to be enough. Everyone had, of course, had a full medical examination, so he did not anticipate any medical trouble. I wondered about this when my own medical exam consisted of peeing into a jar and saying "aah"!

The medicine having been rapidly sorted out, I was told I would have a research project to carry out and that I should now report to Dr Otto Edholm at the Medical Research Council (MRC) division of human physiology, Holly Hill, Hampstead, to sort this out. Sir Raymond Priestly had also touched on the subject of research, and he told me that 4 or 5 kilometres from Halley Bay, there was a rookery of emperor penguins. At the last count there were about ten thousand, but it was difficult to estimate precise numbers. He told me that these birds were close to being the most primitive species of bird and possibly the embryological link in the evolutionary chain between reptiles and birds. They were thus of great scientific importance. There was an anatomist at Charing Cross Hospital who was desperate to get a precisely timed series of emperor penguin embryos at twelve-hour intervals for ten days. He stressed the scientific importance of this and asked me to secure them. Knowing absolutely nothing about emperor penguins but now hopefully moving slowly towards a surgical career, I agreed, for I imagined we were talking about a series of Caesarean sections. It never dawned on me that being birds, they would lay eggs! Nor did he tell me that a previous attempt had been made during Scott's last expedition and that only one man had survived – Apsley Cherry-Garrard.

When I got to the MRC labs in Hampstead, I was told that Dr Harold Lewis looked after the polar research, though I did get a brief interview and a pat on the head from the great Otto Edholm. Harold gave me a desk and a copy of Dr Edholm's book, called *Man in a Cold*

Environment, and told me to go and think of a relevant research project. I read the whole book but was not much wiser at the end than at the beginning on what to do. I had long discussions with lots of people, and I concluded that the concept of acclimatisation to cold was the current subject of most interest. It seems that there were marked physiological changes to be found in response to exposure to a hot environment but virtually no changes had been noted following exposure to a cold climate. I became quite interested in this problem. Since there were indeed changes in animals in response to cold exposure, I thought it would be worth measuring the actual climatic conditions to which polar explorers were exposed during a year in Antarctica. They were not, of course, exposed to the actual climate of the station continuously since they had tents or huts and clothing and external heating. Animals, on the other hand, were naked and had no protection.

The experiment we devised at Hampstead was to observe a selection of men continuously for periods of twenty-four hours. Every fifteen minutes the temperature, humidity, and wind speed were to be measured where they were. In addition the activity in which they were involved during each fifteen-minute period was noted. I set about this with enthusiasm, but I had no research experience, I had no Antarctic experience, and there was little time to read the literature or take advice because I was due to sail in two weeks' time! I was, however, very fortunate to be introduced to Dr Heinz Wolf, who was the bioengineer at Hampstead. He was brilliant and the perfect picture of the mad scientist. He was also a very nice man. He gave me one of his temperature-sensitive vests knitted of thermistor wire. It was worn under the clothing, and temperature measurements were made by plugging it into a Wheatstone bridge, which recorded resistance changes. These were converted to temperature by reference to a calibration chart. The Wheatstone bridge was specially modified by Heinz with a heap of small components which he sent me to a great variety of little shops in London to buy. He also provided me with all sorts of other inventions, such as a watch with a thermometer sticking out of it, which stopped when the temperature fell below zero. The trouble was it did not always start again when the temperature rose above zero. All that plus a hand-held anemometer and a whirling psychrometer, and the polar environmental scientist was ready to begin his main research – except he was not really sure what it was he was trying to achieve. I nearly missed the deadline for delivery of kit to the docks, but at the last minute Major Jim Adam, who was the physiologist to the Army and attached to Otto's unit, appeared and helped to make things happen rapidly so that we just made the deadline.

During this great rush I did manage to get half an hour with Dr Glenister, who repeated his requirement for a series of emperor penguin embryos, which had to be timed at twelve-hour intervals from laying for ten days. He also told me how to dissect an embryo from the yolk of an egg and place it in Bouin's solution. A few days later it was to be transferred to alcohol and sealed until delivery back in the UK. It all sounded pretty straightforward. Surely he must have known what he was requesting – or perhaps he felt that I would not make the attempt to secure the embryos if he told me.

At last I was ready to depart. The last night before reporting to the ship at Southampton, my batman had washed all that I was taking and packed it. I was sitting in the sumptuous Millbank Mess, reading the only copy of the *Daily Mirror* (every other paper was the *Times*) and feeling a bit like Phileas Fogg in the Reform Club before setting out on his celebrated journey around the world in eighty days. I decided on a last special meal to remember and went to Soho (in a bus rather than a carriage), where I entered the famous Pere August's restaurant, and sitting at the bar, I ordered an underdone fillet steak with mushrooms gently sautéed in butter and washed down with a bottle of very fine claret. (I thought I would not need money for a year or so – and it was just as well.) That meal has been in my memory ever since, and I promised myself to repeat it on my return. In the morning, I took the train to Southampton and my adventure began.

Chapter 3

MV *Tottan*

When the cab dropped me at dock 54 of Southampton docks, I had an immediate surge of panic because it was empty. Had I got the date or the time wrong and missed the boat? Closer inspection, however, revealed people I recognised on the dock and a mast sticking up over the edge. The *Tottan* was only 640 tons, and the tide was out, so it was a long way down. It was made to look even smaller because the ship in the next berth was the *Queen Elizabeth* (the first). The *Tottan* was a Norwegian ship with a totally Norwegian crew who spoke very little English. It was a sealing vessel and had been chosen because it was the ship which transported the Royal Society advance party to the Antarctic to establish the base at Halley Bay three years before for the International Geophysical Year. It had reached further south than any British ship since the time when Shackleton lost the *Endurance*. It was under the command of Captain Leif Jacobson – a huge man and a very competent polar navigator and sailor. The mate was an elderly and venerable man called Axel. The crew was friendly, but we could not communicate with them easily. We probably had most to do with the ship's boy, Wendel, because he served the food. I may say that I probably saw least of Wendel because I did not appear in the mess for food very often!

The accommodation was aft but was occupied by the crew. We were accommodated in the forecastle, which was in the bows and consisted of two cabins, each with five berths. We were also allocated one additional cabin aft, but that was given to the base commander, George Lush, and the Royal Society observer, George Hemmen. The reason for the Royal Society's presence was that the base was being taken over by the Falkland Islands Dependencies Survey (FIDS), and a proper Antarctic handover was to take place with George Hemmen returning with the ship and the Royal Society's equipment. The problem with the forecastle was that we had to cross the open deck to get to the main accommodation. If the weather was rough, this could be a problem at mealtimes. Of even greater importance was the fact that the single lavatory in the forecastle had no water, and one had to repair to the stern for such functions as required running water. There was no shower, and there were only two wash basins in the rear area for passengers and crew. The captain had given up his day cabin in the aft accommodation for our use, but there was hardly sitting room for eleven. It was a far cry from the headquarters mess of the Royal Army Medical Corps at Millbank!

We had quite a send-off from relatives and friends. My sister Margaret was there from Cheltenham with her fiancée, Jim Gassor. Commander David Dalgleish, the leader of the advance party expedition also came to wish us well. At precisely 1500 hours on 21 November 1958, the ropes were cast off, and the *Tottan* set sail. I felt elated. I had really wanted to join the Navy, and the heaving deck beneath me was magic. The elation lasted for a full hour until we were leaving Southampton water and I had a growing feeling of foregut discomfort. I was reluctantly forced to admit that this must be seasickness. Still, it has been reported that Nelson was usually sick at the beginning of a voyage, and Hornblower was sick at Spithead when he joined the Navy. I had been so looking forward to trying the brown Norwegian goat's cheese, putting rich condensed milk in my tea, and sampling the various oily fishes. I may say that to this day I have not managed to sample these Scandinavian delicacies from the memory of that voyage.

I retired to my bunk and remained there for the next three days swallowing Avomine tablets twice daily and, to my shame, not offering any to my companions. When I emerged, the sun was shining, and though we were in the middle of the Bay of Biscay, the sea was relatively calm. I tried the experiment of missing my next dose of Avomine.

But the experiment was a failure, and I restarted the treatment and continued till we reached the "silent seventies" of latitude. It was now time to meet the party with whom I was to spend the next year – or two if we were not relieved. I was told that the ship could only get into Halley Bay for about two weeks each year and even that was problematical. That was why we had food for an extra year!

The base commander, George Lush, was a lieutenant in the Royal Navy. He had been the youngest bosun in the Navy, on HMS *Hood*, before being commissioned. He had been present at the establishment of the base and was its main constructor. He knew all about clove hitches and four by two and talked about the "heads" and the "galley". The Army had provided the radio operator, Dennis Savins, the cook, Jim Mace, and the mechanical engineer, Jock Whitehall, from REME. They were all staff sergeants, and, of course, I was from the Army also. FIDS provided Norman Hedderley as the general duty explorer; he had served in the Antarctic in the past and was supposed to keep us right in the exploratory aspects of the job (though he was killed in a climbing accident shortly after he returned home). That completed the support staff, whose function it was to ensure the safe and healthy running of the base as a platform for the work of the scientists.

In order to provide continuity, the Royal Society persuaded one of its party to remain for a further year with us. He was a meteorologist called John Smith. Halley Bay was what is known as a static base, and that meant that its function was to make repeated scientific observations of a largely geophysical nature but not to explore the surroundings. The chief scientist was Mick Blackwell who was a Cambridge graduate in physics with a shining career ahead of him in the meteorological office, while the youngest scientist was a recent physics graduate called Mike Sheret from Edinburgh University whose job was to study the Aurora Australis. Mick Blackwell was assisted by several other meteorologists, including David Limbert, also a member of the advance party, from the met office and two scientists, who had been seconded from the South African Weather Bureau. Gordon Artz and Johannes Bothma were recruited at the last minute. They remembered to grab a South African flag to raise on South Africa Day, but they were on the plane when they remembered they had nothing to toast it with. They therefore bought all the miniatures of the South African liqueur Van der Hum on the plane, and it was duly drunk on South Africa Day when the flag was raised below the Union Jack. They were great colleagues but had very different personalities. Gordon was an extrovert while Johannes was very self-sufficient and quiet. He was a real gentleman. I remember them with affection whenever I can find a glass of Van der Hum after a dinner.

Our main function was to continue the observations made during the International Geophysical Year into what was known as the International Geophysical Corporation and to maintain the base while arrangements were made for it to be taken over by FIDS.

The voyage was meant to allow us to get to know each other and to exchange ideas on what we hoped to achieve. We were a strange bunch – mostly older than the kids that go to the Antarctic nowadays. Mike Sheret was the youngest, and I probably came next. The rest were largely in mid-career, and it was not always clear what they hoped to gain by the experience. The motivation of the scientists was most easy to understand. They were interested in their careers. The same could also be said for the naval base commander, while Norman Hedderley was really a professional explorer and climber. My motivation has already been discussed. While the other Army personnel could also have been thinking of career, all were in very comfortable billets as senior sergeants, which would have provided a much more pleasant life than a year in the Antarctic. We were drawn from widely different intellectual and social backgrounds, and I began to wonder how we would all bed down together for a year in an Antarctic hut.

The *Tottan* provided fat pork and sauerkraut (cabbage boiled in vinegar with caraway seeds) as the staple diet. I never got to taste it because when the weather was calm and I ventured to the mess, the smell always ensured that I had to beat a hasty retreat before I reached the table. The food may have been difficult, but when we reached the tropics and had to sleep five in a cabin without air conditioning or running water, conditions were almost unbearable. George Lush said that crossing the tropics in the *Tottan* was worse than anything we would have to bear during the Antarctic winter, and he was right. The crew erected a hose on the deck and pumped sea water through it, but if you stood under it – which was good – you became all sticky afterwards because there was no fresh water to wash the salt off. I tried sleeping on the forward hold, and that seemed good, but I was just dropping off when I was hit on the face by a flying fish. There were often about half a dozen flying fish on the hold cover in the morning. I started photographing them with my new camera and ended up with three rolls of thirty-six exposure film which showed sea and a dot in the air above.

After a couple of weeks we were in the vicinity of the Canary Islands, and the thought of dry land and a steak was really great. The captain was in a great hurry, however, and we passed by the lights of Las Palmas in the night – the sounds and smells of land so near and yet so far. It was nearly another month before our first land fall, which was Montevideo in Uruguay. It transpired that we would stop there for a full twenty-four hours – big deal. We decided to get off the ship and out of the docks and to spend the night in a hotel. So we asked for the best hotel in Uruguay and proceeded to the Nogoro Hotel. We were discussing who would share a room with whom when someone said, "Look, we have been five to a cabin for the past six weeks. We are only here for one night. So let's have a room each – and one with a private bath." The last was, in fact, a very uncommon luxury in 1958. I will never forget the totally sensuous feeling of slipping into my first bath for six weeks after the tropical experience. I cannot remember a more magnificent sensation – unless it is the lunch we then had at a fantastic restaurant called the Los Aguillas.

We had picked up a little guy called Carlos who insisted on showing us around, took us to all sorts of shops where we were invited to buy a variety of goods usually made of "unborn calf". Jim Mace had been told that the Fray Bentos corned beef factory was in Montevideo, and he was keen to see the process. He had been told it was entirely automatic; it consisted of driving a herd of steers in one end and after only chopping off horns and tail the product emerged at the other end as tins of corned beef. I do not know whether he found the factory. Meanwhile Carlos offered to introduce us to the most lurid, amazing, and unlikely sexual experiences, which would happily occupy the rest of our stay. We had been well warned of the dangers of South America and managed to escape from him before going much further. This was achieved by George Hemmen taking us to the English club to which Antarctic explorers are always welcome. There we met a man who was from Glasgow. He had been a clerk in a city firm, and he was not doing well. He was, in fact, doing so badly that he had been fired. And so in true Glasgow style he had repaired to a hostelry on Clydeside and had proceeded to get well and truly plastered. He remembered nothing else until he had awoken in the hold of a ship. That ship was heading for Montevideo, and so he had remained on board, worked his passage, and lived in South America ever since. He was now a multi-millionaire, and the chairman of a large and successful business in Uruguay. You cannot keep a Glaswegian down. Jock asked him where we could get the biggest steak in town, and he gave us the name of a restaurant and told us to ask for an "entrecote special". We did this with the addition of a bottle of vino tinto national. Jock explained that in his many travels to strange parts of the world he had found it safe to eat almost anything anywhere provided you washed it down with an equal quantity of the local vino. It is a philosophy I have followed through life and have found it effective, so I can recommend it.

After our meal we decided to repair to a night club called the Cubilete, which had been recommended. But when we got there it seemed to be closed because it was in darkness. Since it was all glass, we approached to have a look through the windows and noted that it was in fact a teeming mass of humanity and far from closed, but the lights were almost non-existent. We entered and sat down in a row, each with a young lady in tow. Someone ordered a round of drinks. When the first round of drinks arrived, the waiter, who was wearing dark sunglasses, lit his cigarette lighter to let the man who was paying read the chit. When it came to my turn, I nearly collapsed reading the reckoning, but I paid unflinchingly like a man. Then it was great fun to watch the others as the waiter flashed his lighter. I was still giggling to myself when I noticed that it was nearly my turn again, and so I rapidly suggested that we should perhaps move on. As we moved from night club to night club, various members of our party began to peel off and go to bed. Eventually, only Jock and I were left, and we had an interesting chat on the way home for he was a Glaswegian, too. He was a year or two older than me and had been in a reform school before becoming a boy soldier. He was now in the midst of his first divorce and had taken off to avoid the problems it had caused. When we returned to the hotel and asked for our keys, the clerk looked a bit strange, but only when I was in the lift did I realize why. It was ten past eight in the morning! We were due to sail at twelve, but I thought that having paid good money for the magnificent bed, I would just get in. The next thing I knew was being rudely awakened at ten to twelve, and we caught the boat just in time. It was a terrific twenty-four hours, and I slept for most of the next two days. It now emerged that I was the close buddy of Jock because I had been the only one who had been able to stand the pace and ended the night still following him.

Chapter 4

Port Stanley and the Falkland Isles

It took another week to get to Port Stanley in the Falkland Islands, where the forward station of the Falkland Islands Dependencies Survey was based, administered, and under the ultimate control of the governor. We arrived during the night, and when I came on deck and saw Port Stanley, it appeared just like a Scottish fishing town. The architecture was Scottish, the weather was Scottish, and closer investigation revealed that half the people were called McDonald or McLeod. Glasgow landladies would have loved it, for here mutton to feed students could be acquired for four pence a pound.

We were due to spend a week in Port Stanley including Christmas, but we sailed before the New Year. The first thing we found in Port Stanley was the pub at the head of the pier. There was a wooden bar outside the door to which horses were tied. It was largely a sheep-rearing place, and if you thought the horses outside the door gave the impression of the Wild West, the inside certainly did. There were people dancing on the tables, there were darts flying in all directions, the noise was deafening, and there were at least three fights in progress. It was great fun. When I returned in 1986, I thought I would see if it still existed. I was pleased to find it very little changed despite quarter of a century and a war. When I tentatively peeped inside, I was greeted by a voice which said, "Hello, Doc, how are you doing?"

One of the big things which happened in Port Stanley was that the governor had a cocktail party for all who went south. I was given the task of seeing that Jock got there, but this was not easy because there were four pubs on the way to Government House, and he insisted on stopping at every one, sampling its wares, and having a game with the "arrers". Eventually we arrived. It was a very posh gathering in glittering ambassadorial surroundings, complete with footmen and all the trimmings of the British Raj. The chief medical officer was there as was the colonial secretary. Jock eventually appeared and fortunately behaved himself – must have been his military training.

The chief medical officer, Dr Stuart Slessor, was a very fine man who had made enormous improvements to health care in the Falkland Islands. His calls were made by Land Rover or a horse because there were only 3 or 4 miles of tarred road on the Falkland Islands. The road extended from the jetty at Port Stanley to Government House and had been laid when the Duke of Edinburgh visited the Antarctic in the Royal Yacht *Britannia* in 1956. Dr Slessor was very friendly with the governor and was frequently invited to Government House. He felt that it was not proper to drive to Government House in an old Land Rover, so he had a Rolls Royce imported, which was only used for visiting Government House. The strange thing was that he lived next door, so the Roller merely had to roll down his drive, traverse a few yards of road, and negotiate the drive of Government House!

The cocktail party was on Christmas Eve, and when we left there were all the pubs to negotiate on the way home, so it is hardly surprising that I was looking forward to returning to the ship for a few hours of sleep. As I walked down the jetty, however, I met a colleague, Dr Alex Cumming, coming up. I asked him where he was off to, and he said it was Christmas Day and that he was going to church (it transpired that it was ten o'clock in the morning!). I said I would accompany him, and we entered a beautiful and simple church. The service was very nice, but I felt a bit uncomfortable because I must have been a sight – unshaven and presumably filling the atmosphere with fumes from the degradation products of alcohol. I tried to slink out at the end, but the minister and his wife stopped us and invited us to the manse for a dish of tea and some Christmas cake. This was even more embarrassing since the conversation was all about the evils of drink and the wild parties of the previous night. They were so nice and hospitable that I was truly repentant and left the manse, determined never to place myself in a position like that again. As I walked down the jetty towards the *Tottan* and bed, I met Jock slowly walking up. When I asked him where he was going, he said that he had reckoned that if he proceeded at a sedate pace up the jetty, he would arrive at the door of the pub just as it opened. After thirty seconds of consideration, I agreed to accompany him. And sure enough we arrived at the door of the pub as the clock struck twelve and the door swung open.

The other expedition ship of the day, the RRS *John Biscoe*, was also in port, so there was a large number of Fids about. (Fids was the term used for the Survey's Antarctic base members, and it is still used even though the organisation is now termed the British Antarctic Survey [BAS].) There was a Christmas dance in the town hall, and we all decided to go along. As we approached the hall, a bunch of young local yokels hove into sight, emitting such provocative and insulting remarks as, "Huh, big brave explorers… Think you are tough?… We would soon show you." "Great," I said to myself, rolling up my sleeves and advancing. "I have never been involved in a brawl. This should be great fun." Jock, however, was my minder by this time, and of course much more experienced in the ways of the world than me. He caught me by the shoulder and said, "Doc, away you and look oot yer bandages and just leave this to me."

The visit to Port Stanley lasted for a week. I do not think I could have survived much longer. On the last day, there was a monumental leaving party on the *Tottan*, which cast off in the afternoon heading south exactly a week after we arrived. I think everyone on the Islands was there, and they were all in the captain's day cabin. Port Stanley returned to the "even tenor of its ways" after we left, but it took a couple of days for most of us to surface.

In those days there were no such things as domestic deep freezes – in fact not many households in the UK had a refrigerator. The *Tottan* certainly had no such equipment, and though we would not have much difficulty in freezing and refrigerating food in the Antarctic, we had to get it there first. The stores which we took consisted of tinned and dehydrated food, but in order to have a little fresh meat, we bought a sheep in Port Stanley for a pound (dead, of course), nailed it to the mast, and proceeded south at the full 5-knot top speed of the *Tottan*. I cannot claim that the experiment was an unqualified success.

We headed into the teeth of a real gale but did not really become aware of it till well into the next day when we sobered up. We were heading for our next port of call, which was South Georgia, and that took about another week in rough and featureless seas. We were now aware that it was cold. We arrived at Grytviken, which was impressive. There was an administrative area, a busy whaling station, and a simple monument to Shackleton, who died on the way to South Georgia in 1922. He was buried with the whalers in their cemetery in the area where Shackleton made his greatest contribution – a contribution for which he will always be remembered and will forever maintain the admiration and enthusiasm of those who have a love of achievement and adventure.

Not unlike Port Stanley, Grytviken was largely staffed by a mixture of Scots and Norwegians. Some lived in onshore accommodation, while others lived on an old cruise liner, which came down from Montevideo every season and returned at the end of the summer season. Most of those coming down were there to make money, and the pay was good. The idea was to earn enough to start a business or buy a farm when they returned home, and there were those who achieved that end, but there was a goodly number who never went farther north than Montevideo, where they spent their money in riotous living and had to return south next season to try again.

The Norwegians had the reputation for having difficulty with booze – that is, to stop drinking it when there was any left in the bottle! Alcohol was banned in Grytviken since there was so much heavy machinery about. It was always possible to get some, however, from passing ships. There was a magistrate on Grytviken, and the first couple of Norwegians who were drunk were sentenced to a year of hard labour. They disposed of the garbage, swept the streets, and did all the menial jobs. They locked themselves up at night in the tiny jail and let themselves out in the morning. When their time was served, the administration merely looked around for another couple of drunks to keep the place tidy!

19

There was a tiny shop or slop chest which had sealing knives and Norwegian jerseys; these were reckoned to last a lifetime – a fact which many people will attest to. We all bought jerseys and knives and then set sail from this very rugged but beautiful place. The mountains were huge and impressive, and Mount Paget had not been climbed at that time. The people we met there were very kind and hospitable, but we were in some ways glad to leave because at last we were heading directly for the ice and Halley Bay.

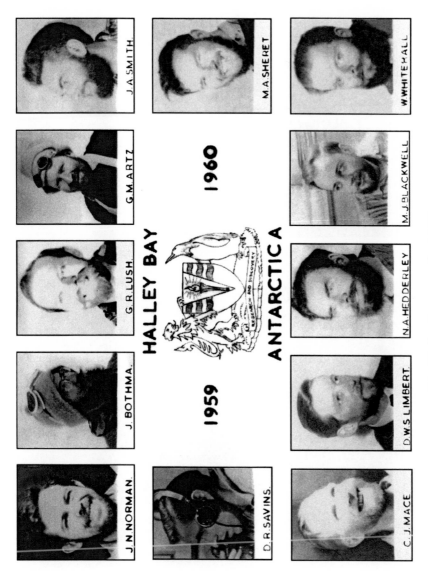

The Halley Bay team for 1959.

21

MV Tottan leaving Southampton, November 1958. Photographer, JP Gassor.

Sir Raymond Priestley demonstrating a specimen of whale bone to HRH the Duke of Edinburgh at Port Lockroy while EMP Salmon looks on. Photographer, AM Carroll, 1956. Reproduced courtesy of NERC-BAS. British Antarctic Survey Archives. Ref. AD6/19/X/27/1.

Sir Vivian Fuchs (right) as a young explorer talking to Ray Aidie at Stonington Island after they returned from a dog sledge trip to the Eklund Islands. Photographer, DG Dalgliesh, 1949. Reproduced courtesy of NERC-BAS. British Antarctic Survey Archives Service. Ref. AD6/19/2/E1316/2.

Port Stanley, Falkland Islands. The cathedral is in the foreground and the Falkland Islands Company on its right. The architecture of the remaining buildings is typically Scottish.

Grytviken, South Georgia. The administration centre is in the foreground while the whaling station can be seen at the deepest aspect of the bay. Shackleton's grave is on the other side of the bay from the administrative buildings.

The plans (dissection area) of the whaling station at Grytviken, South Georgia. A few whale remnants can still be seen. A whole whale could be rendered into its component parts in 10 to 15 minutes.

The liner, used for accommodation, moored to the jetty at Grytviken whaling station. A whale catcher is also seen in he foreground.

Chapter 5

South

We left South Georgia at the end of the second week in January for the last and most exciting leg of our journey. We initially headed southeast since the technique was to pass east of the South Shetland and the South Sandwich Islands before turning south to approach the Weddell Sea pack ice about Cap Norwegia. At that point there was usually what was known as a shore lead of clear water between the Weddell pack ice and the continental ice shelf. This had been discovered and proved when Captain Jacobsen made his very successful journey to establish the advance party for the IGY at Halley Bay three years previously. Indeed, during the same year the Magga Dan had tried to plunge straight across the Weddell pack to establish the advance party of Sir Vivian Fuchs' Trans-Antarctic Expedition (TAE) a little further down the Caird Coast and had become beset for several weeks. The result was that the advance party of TAE was not able to get its living quarters built or its stores unpacked before winter set in, and the party had to spend the whole Antarctic winter in a converted packing case! In addition, they lost much of their stores because the ship had to depart almost as soon as it arrived so that it could get back out.

As we proceeded south it became colder, and we began to see bits of floating ice, then small bergs, and finally large bergs. Visibility was good, and it was summer, so there was plenty of light. Remembering the *Titanic*, I had thought that there would be a great problem and worry about icebergs, but no one seemed to be very concerned. In the north, of course, the mists of winter and the darkness made the whole situation much more dangerous. The other big advantage of moving south was that the sea became progressively more calm as the amount of ice increased, and I was thus able to take a greater interest in my surroundings. The old salts talk about the roaring forties, the terrible fifties, the screaming sixties, and the silent seventies, and I can confirm this to be a true observation.

As we approached the pack ice, the whole company seemed to come alive, and I wondered whether anyone would really ascend the very high mast to the crow's nest. I was left in little doubt, because the captain sent for me and pointed out a fairly large cavity in one of his teeth, saying that the cold winds made this very painful when he was in the crow's nest. I, therefore, made up a paste of clove oil and some solid and filled the cavity. He was quite pleased and said in his commanding but poor English, "You sit". So I sat. He then turned to a locker and took out a bottle of whisky and two tumblers, put them on the table between us, pulled out the cork, and threw it out the window. I was not sure whether that was a good sign. He said, "Have drink." I duly helped myself to a modest portion of whisky, whereupon he picked up the bottle and, filling my tumbler to the brim, said, "I said, you have drink". I cannot really remember how the meeting ended!

Eventually, we came towards a solid sheet of ice, and by this time the captain was in the crow's nest. He remained there for four days and four nights since there was twenty-four hours of light by this time. We had already dodged between fairly large sheets of ice, but on this occasion there seemed to be no gap, so I wondered what we would do. What actually happened was that we went to full speed and barged straight into the ice. The bow came up over the ice and rode over it, crushing it. The noise was terrible, and the ship moved violently in all directions as it proceeded with great sheets of ice riding up as far as the deck and the sounds of crashing crockery from below. I hung on to the rail open-mouthed. This was certainly not what I had expected.

We were now truly getting somewhere! After a couple of days like this – reversing and going forward, occasionally getting stuck, and then having another go – we landed in progressively larger lakes in the ice until, having entered the famous shore lead, we were once again in clear water. It was now plain sailing until we reached Halley Bay. It was not quite so good for those whom we relieved, for they were beset for many days and had to get over the side and dig the ship out from time to time with the aid of bamboo poles and carefully placed charges of dynamite!

All the way down the lead, there was an unbroken ice cliff about 200 feet high until we came to Halley Bay, where there was an observable slope up to the top of the cliff. The weather was fine, and the sea mercifully calm. But I could well imagine the concern of the advance party three years before as they spent day after day sailing down this lead and looking for a means to gain access to the continent. They even considered the possibility of scaling the cliff and bringing the stores ashore by rigging some form of pulley system. The cliffs were, in fact, not the continent but an ice shelf (the Brunt Ice Shelf). It was floating and was hinged to the main continent about 200 miles inland by a glacier (the Dawson-Lambton Glacier). Eventually, they came to an indentation where there was a slope up to the ice shelf, and even though they were not quite as far south as they had hoped, they elected to settle on a landing there and called it Halley Bay. When we arrived, the only thing I saw was an indentation with some sea ice and a few chaps with a Ferguson tractor on it. I suppose if Captain Jacobson had not been there before and the chaps had not come to the sea ice, we could have missed it!

Chapter 6

Halley Bay

The first thing to be done was to anchor the ship. This was achieved by dragging a hawser across the ice for about 100 yards and digging a hole in the ice for an anchor, which was a balk of timber attached to the hawser. This was very hard work, for sea ice is enormously hard. The sun was shining, however, and the temperature was a full degree Celsius. The crew certainly had loads of help, for the Royal Society party was anxious to see that the boat remained where it was! They had been at Halley Bay for two years, and there was no certainty that the ship would get through. After all we were in the vicinity of the area where the *Endurance* was lost. During this year, one of the other bases was not relieved, and that is why each base had food for two years. The plight of the advance party of Sir Vivian Fuchs' Trans-Antarctic Expedition (TAE) was still very fresh in their minds, since its base at Vassel Bay was only a short way down the Caird Coast. It was indeed so close that the TAE doctor had been able to visit Halley Bay when the Royal Society doctor, Colonel Smart, had an accident and needed medical help. The TAE ship, *Magga Dan*, had been able to get back out without too much difficulty despite her horrendous experience, when she attempted to proceed straight across the Weddell pack ice on the way in. Such experiences made us realize how fortunate we were to have had a relatively trouble-free and pleasant passage through the ice and fully explained the relief of the Royal Society party when we arrived on time.

There was an enormous amount of gear to unload, for a new organization was taking over the base, and the Royal Society was taking most of its equipment back. Equally, Captain Jacobsen did not want to hang about as the lead would likely be open for a few weeks only. He was also anxious to get back north to Halifax for the sealing. Since *Tottan* was beset for a time on the way out, she did, in fact, only just make it back on schedule. When she got back to Southampton and was examined for damage, it was found that the rivets on the bow were worn smooth, and it was a surprise that none had sprung!

There were three Ferguson farm tractors available for unloading, and this immediately commenced after only the briefest introductions to our opposite numbers. Each tractor could pull two large Maudheim sledges, and it took about three-quarters of an hour to load them, another half hour across sea ice to achieve the top of the slope to the ice shelf, and then about an hour to reach the base, unload, and begin the return journey. Since time was at a premium, we worked through the twenty-four hours either unloading on the ship or at the base; then the Royal Society equipment had to be loaded. It took us about ten days before the ship was ready to sail. I had had difficulty in growing a beard because I could get no further than four days, when it became so uncomfortable and scruffy that I had to shave. At the end of ten days of very hard manual work and with very little time for sleep, I found I had a beard which I had not noticed growing!

I was based on the ship, while the doctor I was relieving, Bert Brooker, was at the base. About forty years later I read a book by the Royal Society's base commander, where he noted that the outgoing doctor had sustained a fairly nasty injury during the relief which he had had to deal with himself. Obviously he had not remembered that there was a doctor on the ship – or possibly he thought I was a navvy! Perhaps he was just pointing out that he was now so good at everything that medicine held no secrets from him!

The weather was very good for most of the unloading period, and the sun shone upon us twenty-four hours of the day. The atmosphere was so rarefied, however, that many of the men got severely sunburned. This was not something I expected in the Antarctic. I saw worse cases of severe sunburn in the Antarctic than I have ever seen elsewhere.

Fortunately, we were provided with plenty of sunscreen, but so intense was the work that it was often not applied. Sunscreen application was only forgotten once by each man since the resulting burns were very painful indeed. We were largely novices, of course, and must have looked as odd walking about in our split new Antarctic gear as our relief crew looked to us a year later. The old hands in our party wore their old togs from what they always termed the "first year" so as not to be confused with the new boys. The gear we were issued impressed me greatly for I had not seen windproof clothing in the UK in the 1950s. During the first blow, I felt really emancipated to be able to walk about in comfort in a jersey covered with a very light-weight windproof anorak.

Some of us did make stupid mistakes from ignorance. The surface of the ice shelf was flat, and nature apparently required it to remain so. When there was a blizzard, the surface snow swirled and drifted, levelling the surface out. If anything was left sticking up above the surface, it soon became buried. Thus even the buildings were soon buried, and the base appeared as a level snowfield. We had to be careful not to leave anything protruding above the surface. If anything was left, for example, a tractor, it had to be dug out after the blow. One of our party left a large collection of bamboo stakes sticking into the surface before a blizzard. They were about twenty-feet high, and after the blizzard the whole topography of the base was altered. They were smoothly buried and anything near them was about twenty-feet down. The culprit was unpopular, and he did not do it again. I remember he was not a new boy but one from "the first year". Many of these things had to be learned quickly, and there had to be a fairly steep learning curve to prevent accidents. That is why FIDS tried to make people stay for two years so that only half of the base is relieved each year. This ensured that at least half of the personnel had some experience and prevented the newcomers from doing stupid or dangerous things.

Since I was based on the ship and the unloading commenced immediately, I had not seen the base which was some way inland on the ice shelf. This was judged to be necessary so that if a chunk of the ice shelf broke off during a blizzard and became an iceberg, it would be less likely to include us. After a couple of days, however, the weather deteriorated sufficiently to cause a pause in the unloading. Mike Sheret and I jumped on the last load to leave and rode up to the base. When we arrived at the top of the slope, all that could be seen was an endless stretch of snow and ice with no features whatsoever. An hour later we arrived at the base. There was not much more to be seen, for everything was buried by snow and ice. All that could be seen of the living quarters were a few aerials and chimneys. There was a hatch and a ladder that disappeared down a shaft about thirty feet to the bottom. We descended cautiously and arrived at the front door. On entering, we were somewhat surprised to find a wide corridor. It was comfortably warm, and at the end of it we found the kitchen. The duty cook was clearing up after a meal, and he was alone. We asked him if he had anything kind of British to eat. He said it was all cleared away and that he could only offer us beans on toast as that was all that was readily available. We were delighted, for after a couple of months of fiskeballe, fat mutton, and sauerkraut it tasted to me as good as the fantastic steak at Pere August's on the night before sailing or the lunch at Los Aguillas in Montevideo. Our admiration for the magnificent seamanship of the Norwegians did not extend to what they gave us to eat!

By 1950 Antarctic standards, the hut was quite palatial. Most huts consisted of one room with four or five bunks built into the walls, while there was space allocated for cooking, recreation, report writing, communications, and some scientific work. In some cases an additional room was provided as a lab. The Halley hut was two- or three-hundred-feet long, had a well-appointed kitchen and dining room, a very comfortable lounge, two large and well-heated bunk rooms, and a bathroom. There were several work rooms, in addition, for the scientists, and a large and well-equipped dark room for photography. There was also a radio shack and a surgery, while, in the loft, there was plenty of space for storage and for carving out additional little offices or meeting rooms. Further investigation revealed a number of additional peripheral buildings, such as a geomagnetic laboratory, a dexion tower for the all-sky camera to photograph the Aurora Australis, a hut to house the equipment to make hydrogen for the weather balloons, and a radar set to follow them. There was also equipment to measure the thickness of the ozone layer – the very equipment which detected the hole in the ozone layer many years later. This was housed within a small hut of its own mounted on skis. The idea was that it could be moved after blizzards to keep it on the surface. This was the beginning of the thinking about how to maintain buildings at Halley Bay. The hut and the equipment were looked after by John Smith. These were all new sciences to me, and I looked forward to finding out about them since I knew virtually nothing about any of them at that time. This was, however, not the time to ask questions. There was so much urgent work to be done. After a quick look around the base, we returned to the ship and the toil in the hold.

The weather was excellent for the first week of unloading. A day or so after our return from the base, we were engrossed in unloading in the hold but soon became aware of rising wind. The weather deteriorated rapidly as the wind velocity increased. The cargo started moving as the motion of the ship increased. When a large box slid rapidly across the hold and smashed into the other side, we concluded that we were in some danger and climbed out of the hold to see what was going on. When we reached the deck, the wind velocity was about 20 knots. This was enough to cause the snow on the ice shelf to drift and swirl to such an extent that the outline of the cliff could no longer be seen, and even the position of the slope was difficult to identify. A loaded sledge had just taken off for the slope, and it was decided to suspend work for the time being. Mike and I thought the conditions were not all that bad. But we were not aware of the effect which that wind speed had on visibility on the ice shelf. This could result in a tractor losing direction and driving off into the wide blue yonder, or worse still, driving over the edge of the cliff. A year later, during the relief, I was driving an empty sledge back to the ship in a wind speed of about 15 knots when I became aware that the tracks of previous vehicles, which I was following, were difficult to see. Since there were no other visible landmarks, I stopped and walked to the front of the tractor to determine whether I could see the tracks of previous sledges. I did not see any tracks, but as I peered ahead I found that I had stopped right on the edge of a 200-foot cliff overlooking the sea ice. That was, in my view, a good example of the presence of a guardian angel!

In any event, conditions were not that bad on the sea ice, and the bosun and another seaman went off to investigate the sea anchor.

Another couple strolled off to have a look at a Weddell seal sleeping on the ice. Another two or three men were dispatched to pick up some boxes that had fallen off previous sledges. I merely leant on the rail and observed Antarctica and the developing storm, which showed no signs of abating. It seemed to me that the sea ice had begun to move up and down. The captain must have noticed this at about the same time, for he gave a couple of blasts on the whistle and waved to those on the ice to return. With dramatic suddenness great cracks appeared on the sea ice, and slowly these began to widen. It seemed clear that the sea ice was breaking up. Yet the tractor was only about three-quarters of the way to the shelf, and several groups of people were scattered over the ice. The various groups and individuals jumped over the widening cracks to get to the biggest floes and those nearest the ship. Meanwhile the tractor continued at its flat-out speed of about 15 miles per hour. It crossed one crack and was proceeding towards the next, which seemed to be widening all the time. Meanwhile the ship's engines were started, and the anchor cable was cut with an axe.

The wind increased in noise and soon became a true blizzard. The floes began to separate and swirl so that at least half a dozen groups or individuals were on different swirling floes which seemed intent on going to sea. Fortunately the tractor and sledge made it over the last crack and onto the slope and reached the safety of the ice shelf. I was transfixed and could not see how we could avoid losing several of the ship's crew. We then saw a magnificent display of Captain Jacobsen's seamanship as he steered the *Tottan* through this dangerous sea of rapidly moving jagged ice floes. The first couple of rescues were reasonably straightforward though the launching of the chaps at the passing scrambling net was a bit hair-raising. The last man seemed to be disappearing into the murk. However, as the wind rose, visibility deteriorated, and the movement of the great mass of very hard ice rapidly increased. Indeed I wondered whether a collision between the floe and the *Tottan* would not breach the *Tottan*. In the nick of time, however, the ship caught up with the floe, and the man jumped across the gap, caught the scrambling net, and reached the deck. We lost several boxes of equipment, but most of it was Royal Society equipment being returned to the UK; the new stuff was usually loaded directly onto the sledges. Mercifully, however, there was no loss of life – though some of those on the floes may have wished they were wearing brown trousers!

I was isolated on the ship, which then steamed offshore to ride out the storm. The gale had rapidly developed into a typical Antarctic blizzard, which raged on for the next three days. The ice shelf was totally concealed. I took the opportunity to attend to a carbuncle on the ankle of the radio operator – partly caused, I am sure, because I had failed to get enough antibiotic from the captain in the first instance. He was apparently keeping it for the sealing, for specfinger (chronic infection following seal bite) is difficult to manage and renders a person less able to cull the seals. I incised the radio operator's carbuncle and evacuated lots of pus. He was relieved, and I was pleased to return to my profession albeit only fleetingly. His attendants invited me to have a drink, and, remembering the aftermath of the captain's dentistry, I politely declined. I was pushed, but I persistently declined. They then apparently remembered my abortive attempts to obtain strawberries and cream in Montevideo (where I eventually received Turkish coffee instead!) and said it would be impolite to go off without something. So they offered me a glass of strawberry juice. I agreed, and it was indeed good. Halfway through the third glass I was aware of a glint in the eye of the third engineer who had joined us and then realized that the drink had been spiked with puro.

I do not know what puro is, but it smells like absolute alcohol and has the same effect. When I rejoined my colleagues on the upper deck, at least another day had passed and the blizzard was blowing itself out. The sea ice had all blown away, and we were able to anchor directly to the ice shelf halfway up the slope. Thereafter, the unloading proceeded without further ado and much faster, for the distance to the base had been cut down by over a mile and a half. The process was concluded only one day after schedule, so the Royal Society party were not held up. There was, however, one last monumental party on the ship (courtesy of the Royal Society) and one at the base (courtesy of FIDS) before *Tottan* was able to leave, which she did during the last week of January.

We all went down to the bay to wave good-bye to *Tottan*, as she sailed into the wide blue yonder, leaving the ten of us behind on the ice. I remember a feeling of great loneliness and wonder at what the future would hold – whether I would be able to cope with what was required during the coming year in this place from where there was no escape and how we would all get on with each other. Strangely, I was not in the least concerned about my ability to cope with any medical problems which might arise. Such is the confidence of youth!

Chapter 7

Life at Halley Bay

When the ship left, there were stores lying about everywhere – both inside and outside the hut. Everyone seemed very busy getting to grips with their own area. Even so, it did seem very quiet, presumably because we were now a small party and alone. Also, I think most of us were glad to see the back of the ship so that we could spread out and get to work instead of being unable to organise our work areas. We were required to spend much valuable time socialising with the ship's crew or the outgoing party whose work was essentially done. After checking my medical stores and constructing the surgery, which was a small area in the roof space, I did not have too much to do because no one seemed to be sick. I was, therefore, available and called upon by all and sundry when they needed a hand to lift heavy boxes. Indeed, when we were sitting in the lounge having a cup of tea one afternoon, the cook came fussing in, looked around the assembled personnel, and said in a quiet voice, "Doc, could I have a word with you, please?" Sensing at last the possibility of exercising my professional skills, I duly withdrew. When outside, he said in a conspiratorial voice, "I would like you to take these boxes of tinned fruit and stow them in the loft!"

The hut had been built three years before by the Royal Society Advance party. It was very well built and spacious enough for ten men, certainly by the standards of an 1950s Antarctic hut. The Royal Society party was more than twice the size of ours since we were largely a caretaker party whose main function was really to keep the place going until the programmes and personnel of the new organization were established. The hut was, however, completely buried by drifting snow. The common entrance was by the back door – a hatch in the roof which took one into the loft space. The thirty-foot shaft down to the front door was rarely used, but it was necessary to keep it clear in case of fire. On arrival at the base, all you could see was a packing case, which was the "back door" in the roof, and a few chimneys of metal. The hut was heated by coal-fired Esse stoves; the cooking range in the kitchen was also fired by coal. Every time there was a blizzard (and there were two or three per month), everything was buried deep, and we had to go round putting extensions on the chimneys and the back door (usually by adding yet another radiosonde packing case). It was, however, very cosy inside and indeed there were large stoves in the two bunkrooms. It was in fact much more comfortable than the bedrooms at home in these pre-central-heating days.

We had a large copper tank beside the range in the kitchen for water, and the technique was that the duty "gash hand" shovelled snow down a shoot leading to the tank twice a day. Many years later, there was an outbreak of recurrent diarrhoea and vomiting at one of the bases on the Antarctic peninsula. The cause was difficult to determine since food hygiene was good. A clue came from the observation that these outbreaks were usually at the weekends. There was usually a big clean-up of the hut at that time followed by a party, but the cause was apparently not hangovers as someone rather cruelly suggested. Further detailed inquiry revealed that it was the practice to feed the sea birds with the scraps remaining after meals. There was a high use of water at the weekends and any contaminants in the water probably reached a high concentration at the weekends. Moreover, it was further revealed that Skua gulls could carry Salmonella in their gut as modern poultry often do. These birds usually ate what was available until they had difficulty in taking off, and they usually excreted the excess weight to give them "lift off" (which earned them the local, rather crude sobriquet of "Shite Hawks"). Whether the contamination of the snow subsequently shovelled down the water shoot was the cause of the problem or not, there were no further episodes of food poisoning when the practice of feeding the gulls ceased. In Halley there were, however, no sea birds during summer, so mercifully we were at least spared that hazard.

There was a smaller version of the kitchen shoot above a tank beside the bathroom. This provided us with hot water, for there was an associated coal-fired stove alongside. We were allowed a bath once a week when we did our laundry (doby!) – usually before bathing in the same water. This luxury was afforded to the "gash hand". The clothes dried in about half an hour since the humidity was so low (about 20 per cent relative humidity). This, of course, meant that the hut was very inflammable; there was always a night watchman on duty. But even with a night watchman, there have been very few survivors following fires in Antarctic huts. On most well-appointed bases, there was an auxiliary hut some distance from the main hut for such an eventuality. Also, sufficient extra food was provided for a year in case the relief ship failed to reach the base. This was usually kept in a dump, well away from the main living hut against the risk of fire.

You may be wondering what a gash hand is. The use of the term derives from the long naval history of Antarctic exploration. The base commander of the advance party was Commander David Dalgleish RN, and he was accompanied by a remarkable man, George Lush, the former bosun of HMS *Hood*. George was now our base leader – hence the use of terms like "gash" for rubbish and "gash hand" for the duty domestic. We talked about the galley and slept in bunks, and when we needed to pass water, we went to the heads. The heads were quite remarkable. Originally a forty-gallon oil drum was used, and this had to be manhandled outside when it was full. The same was done with the bath water. When you stuck your head out of the hut with a bucket of hot water after a bath, there was the most amazing sensation of your hair standing on end. Presumably the water on the hair immediately froze.

These manoeuvres became progressively more difficult as the hut became more and more deeply buried by snow. You can imagine the struggle (and the language) when faced with trying to take a forty-gallon drum of shit through a small hole in the roof or up a thirty-foot ladder! During a blizzard when the drum needed emptying, someone eventually hit on the idea of knocking the bottom out of a drum and pouring several buckets of hot water down to create a cavern. Thereafter, we just used the same drum and poured the bath water down each day.

It worked well. Eventually, we would just pull the plug out of the bath and that emptied it just as well. I did notice an ammoniacal smell at the other end of the hut on occasion, however, and wondered whether we were all going to disappear into a sea of slurry one day!

The "heads" was the only room which was not heated, though there was a very small oil-fired greenhouse heater to maintain the temperature just below freezing. This had the advantage of making it reasonably comfortable for use, but not too comfortable to encourage base members to take a book with them. There was a side vent let into the drum, which must have been added by an explorer who had been a plumber in civilian life. This was presumably to allow the escape of noxious gases and it worked well. When there was a blizzard, you could hear the wind gusting and moaning over this tube. It was arranged to suit the prevailing wind. But on rare occasions, when the wind came from the opposite direction, it could gust down the tube and then up the drum. The occasional blast of wind at −40 degrees could be somewhat uncomfortable, to say the least, and encouraged the development of quick-release equipment!

One of the other very fine parts of this hut was the lounge which had been lovingly constructed by George Lush and his mates during the winter of the first year. There was a bar at one end and a library at the other. The first thing George did when he arrived was to take down the book at the top right-hand corner – volume one of Gibbons' *Decline and Fall of the Roman Empire*. "Just as I thought," he said. "It has not been moved since I put it there three years ago!" In the centre of one wall was a beautifully carved mock Tudor fireplace with the motto above: "Mon Dieu Rhone Feu Que Pince Nez" – a very appropriate motto for such a place, as people came to realize more and more.

As far as the bar was concerned, we had taken a reasonable amount of booze down with us, thanks to the foresight of those who had been south before (the first year); the occasional party is essential for survival on such a posting. We had some fine wine so that we could have a glass of wine with our dinner on a Saturday night when we dressed up. George Lush tended to run the base a bit like a naval establishment – but not with rigid destroyer discipline as Captain Scott had. As soon as the Royal Society party had left and the base was secured, he decreed that it would be scrubbed out from stem to stern. We spent the morning on our knees scrubbing the floors and polishing the furniture – and indeed every Saturday morning thereafter. On Saturday evenings, we dressed up in our best European suits and gathered in the lounge for a drink before dinner, which was accompanied by a bottle of wine. After dinner we repaired back to the lounge for a film show. We had a bit of a struggle to persuade the Royal Society to leave the cine-projector. We succeeded but failed to persuade them to leave many films. Among those which we managed to retain, the best was undoubtedly the *Three Musketeers*. We saw it so many times that we could almost repeat the dialogue. Eventually, we played it backwards to great effect. There is a scene where D'Artagnon is fencing with the captain of the cardinal's guard at the top of a staircase. When he cuts the captain's braces, his trousers fall to his ankles and he somersaults to the bottom of the stairs. When it is played backwards, the captain of the cardinal's guard somersaults up to the top of the stairs and his trousers rise to their correct position before he starts his desperate sword fight. The other films were almost entirely set in women's prisons, which was not the most exciting type of entertainment for us.

We had enough booze to allow a gin and tonic before dinner on most nights. As time passed this seemed to have a progressively inebriating effect so that one was quite happy during dinner but had a mini-hangover for an hour or so afterwards. I wondered whether this could have had something to do with the very dry atmosphere and whether we were mildly dehydrated most of the time. We also had enough wine for birthdays and the big celebrations of Christmas and Midwinter. It was, of course, all exported duty free, and I do not remember contributing much money. But perhaps FIDS and people like George Lush and other old polar hands put in a contribution. On the other hand, I also remember that duty free gin cost eight shillings a bottle!

The hut was built upon an ice shelf, which was in fact floating though attached at that time to the main continent by the Dawson-Lampton Glacier about 200 miles away. Though it was not moving perceptibly, we were in fact heading north at a rate of a few yards per annum. As the hut became buried it was distorted by the different ice

41

pressures applied around it and also by differential melting of the ice around warmer and colder parts of the hut. This meant that you had to walk uphill in certain parts. In parts there was quite some space around the hut where the ice had melted. On a Saturday night, you could open one of the leaded windows in the lounge and break off a bit of ice stalagmite for your gin and tonic! Many years later the hut moved so close to the edge of the ice shelf that it was eventually seen being discharged through the side of the shelf and into the Weddell Sea. Several other huts were subsequently built taking note of the problems of previous constructions. One concept involved building the various huts within giant cylinders to prevent differential ice pressures from distorting the buildings. Another was built 40 miles inland to avoid the problems of being too close to the edge of the ice shelf. At that point the name of the base was changed to Halley since there was no longer an associated bay. The Survey is now at Halley 5, and Halley 6 is being built. The current idea is to use the oil rig jack-up principle. The various buildings are built on a platform, which has legs at each corner like an oil rig and when it begins to sink, the legs are wound up like those of an oil rig so that it is kept at the required level. It was certainly hard labour to wind up the legs of Halley 5, but it was said that Halley 6 will rise from the drift by the press of a button!

As we bedded down, it was interesting to watch the development of interpersonal relationships. We were ten men from totally different social and cultural backgrounds and had the full range of intellectual attainments. There were roughly two groups: the scientists and the support personnel. The support personnel were undoubtedly the top dogs at first because they could cope with all the physical and structural needs of the base while the scientists were often out of their depth in these areas – like leaving a wall of upright bamboo stakes outside during a blizzard. The scientists were mildly bullied at first, but it was interesting to see the intellectual superiority of the scientists triumphing in the end. The turning came one Saturday night when we were having our weekly dinner and film show – an occasion when we all put on a suit and tried to appear civilised. The cook came in, looked disparagingly at the chief scientist's suit, and said, "Huh, twenty quid at Montague Burton's, I suppose". Mick Blackwell answered, "My dear Charlie, you wouldn't get this quality for twenty quid!" Charlie was completely thrown and did not know how to respond. That was the beginning of the scientific revival. As medical officer I was placed midway between the groups which was an interesting position.

The behaviour of some people did not change at all during the year while others tended to lose the veneer of polite behaviour, which is necessary to live in a civilised community. All soon learned, however, that in a small, close-knit community, it was necessary to practice much more rigid personal discipline to survive. If you fell out with someone, you still had to meet him at breakfast next morning and that could be unpleasant. Also, we all became very touchy as time passed, and a minor remark in bad taste could cause terrible offence. This did not matter much when we were all very busy. But as the tasks became repetitive and less time was needed for them, we were thrown together more and more. Particular personality traits – such as the know-all – could really get on your nerves unless you were of a very phlegmatic and laid-back personality yourself. We also soon found that repetitive behaviour could also drive one up the wall. For example, one of our number had a particular way of saying good morning three times as he entered the dining room for breakfast. It was funny at first, but when it was repeated day after day for weeks on end, you had to grind your teeth to avoid hitting him! Such personality problems were much more marked on a static base, such as ours, where the work was repetitive and observations had to be made "every hour on the hour". On the bases where travelling took place, there was a variation of activity and something new to discuss as base members went off on their explorations and returned with stories and new experiences.

Chapter 8

Work at Halley Bay

Since there did not seem to be much medicine to be attended to and the others were so busy setting up their equipment and learning how it worked in this strange environment, I asked George Lush if he needed an assistant. He readily accepted my offer. That was the first of my second jobs which I took on to pass the time, to help the others, and to learn new skills. George was busy at this time bringing the maintenance of the base up to standard and securing it for winter. There was a second doorway into the hut on the other side that was not in use, and George thought it should be dug out to serve as a fire escape. This meant digging out another thirty-foot shaft from the surface down to the door, and it took several days. It was good exercise, and I enjoyed the effort. It also gave me a real sense of achievement. George lined the shaft with plywood, installed a ladder, and put a hatch on top. I was really proud of the result and the relatively short time it took to complete. When that was done, we dug a second shaft close to the kitchen and erected a kind of block and tackle affair so that large items could be brought directly in and out. The idea behind this may have been to allow the sewage to be winched up to the surface. But we had solved that problem by that time so that it was only used to bring in supplies from the food dumps and to remove rubbish. For that purpose it was very effective.

This phase was busy and quiet as the various scientists and support personnel got to grips with their individual areas of responsibility.

We were tired at night, and all had problems to sort out. I built an operating table of dexion, but there was not much surgery to perform. It was quite useful, however, for a snooze after lunch! I also had to start my medical research, which required the recruitment of four subjects who would be followed around for twenty-four hour periods once a month. I had made some tentative approaches during the voyage, and I needed to start right away, but everyone was so busy with their own problems that it was not easy. I had to choose subjects who were not only willing but who would stay the course through the long, difficult times of winter. This required judgement, but I did not know them well enough to make reasonable choices. I did not appreciate this at the time, but fortunately those I chose were good subjects and stayed the course.

After setting up my surgery, arranging all my pills and potions on the shelves, and building my operating table, there did not seem to be much medicine to do. Everyone else was extraordinarily busy, and I suppose I felt a bit like the girl who "took her harp to a party and no one asked her to play". I, therefore, became involved in all sorts of jobs to pass the time, to help the others, to learn new skills, and hopefully to encourage recruitment of subjects for my research.

The big event of the day was the launch of the weather balloon, and a very early start had to be made by the chap who went to the balloon shed to make hydrogen and to fill the balloon. This entailed a kind of enormous Kipps apparatus into which was poured ground marble chips followed by acid. You had to stand well clear, in case there was ice blocking the system and it blew back. It took some time to fill the balloon. When this was done, an instrument called a radiosonde was attached by a string to the balloon and it was then launched. As it ascended it measured temperature and pressure, and it was tracked by radar so that its height and direction could be measured every few minutes until the balloon burst an hour or so later. This allowed the wind velocity and direction to be calculated at the various heights. Since the Antarctic is regarded as a key area in the development of weather systems, these measurements were very important not only for weather forecasting but for research into the development of weather systems.

Like everything else, the balloon shed was buried by drifting snow, and when the launch took place, one had to climb out of a fairly deep hole for a start. That was fine unless there was a high wind blowing, since this caught the balloon as soon as it began to appear out of the hole in the ground. When the wind caught the massive balloon, it moved horizontally and the sonde crashed into the ground and was destroyed. In order to prevent the balloon shed from being further buried by drifting snow, the large opening was covered by two huge doors made of plywood. These flaps were opened by a pulley system only when a balloon was to be launched. It was a bit like the system designed by Ernst Stavros Bloefeld for launching the Moonraker missiles in the James Bond film of that name.

The doors prevented the balloon shed from being further buried, but they did not prevent the balloon from going nearly horizontal in high winds and smashing the sonde into the ice shelf. Some help was gained by shortening the string, which attached the balloon to the sonde. But we soon found that it was difficult to launch a weather balloon successfully if the wind speed was greater than 12 or 15 knots. The final trick was to use me. As a budding surgeon I was reckoned to be in a position to tie knots faster than the others. I lay flat at the mouth of the hole from which the sonde would emerge with my hands in electrically heated gloves. As the man launching the balloon rushed up the steps from the hole, I withdrew my heated hands as he passed me, caught the shortened string from the balloon, and tied it to the string on the sonde in a continuous movement. He then threw the sonde upwards. It was all very exciting – especially when it worked – and allowed us to launch balloons unless there was a real blizzard raging. That not only gave us the ability to launch at higher wind speeds. Also it was great for morale since there was much excitement at the launch.

Nowadays, there is a mobile balloon shed above the surface, and the balloon is filled from cylinders of hydrogen. There is little problem about achieving a launch in bad weather since it is possible to release the balloon from a height. They just open the roof and release it. I cannot help thinking, however, that something is lost by making it easy and removing the challenge. But I am sure it is better for science. The sonde was followed by radar until the balloon burst. And another of my jobs was as radar operator number two. After the launch I had to run as fast as possible to the Decca radar and site it on the balloon by means of a kind of gun site. Gordon Artz was the radar operator, and I had to shout up, down, right, left until he picked up the reflector of the sonde on his screen – if possible before the balloon disappeared through the cloud base. We spent the next two hours happily following the sonde and making measurements of temperature, azimuth, and height every two minutes until the balloon burst. The meteorologists then spent the rest of the morning working out the results before radioing them off to the "met." office in UK, and I went for breakfast. When the sonde settled down, Gordon and I had many a long philosophic discussion in the peace and warmth of the radar cabin.

I was also diesel mechanic number two, and I enjoyed working with Jock Whitehall who was, as I have said, a staff sergeant in REME and a Glaswegian. The base was powered by two great Meadows diesel-electric generators which ran on aviation fuel. The generator shed was a little distance from the main living quarters but at one time was connected by a wooden passageway. Immediate access to the generators was vital since power was needed for the continuous-recording scientific apparatus. This passageway was, however, soon buried in the drifting snow – probably the first blizzard after its construction – and it was now an ice tunnel joining the living quarters to the generators. There were two generators, but only one was run at a time since that was sufficient for the needs of the base. The forty-gallon fuel drums were based outside, and the fuel was pumped down to a tank in the shed, which held about a three-day supply.

Sometimes in a bad blow, it was nearly impossible to reach the fuel dump, but we always managed it eventually – albeit on one occasion it was touch and go. The problem was that in a unidirectional blow at wind speeds greater than 70 knots, a kind of venturi effect is caused if you turn your back to the wind, and there is no air to breathe in front of you. Equally, if you face the wind, you cannot see where you are going for the sheer force of the wind and the drifting snow. I thought I had the answer by putting a polythene bag over my head to protect my face. When I stepped into the wind, the polythene was so closely applied to my face that I nearly suffocated, and it was very difficult to remove the bag. That was, of course, before the statements about protecting children from such hazards were issued. When these warnings appeared many years later, I remembered the real panic caused by my experiment.

Twice during the year, we carried out maintenance on the generators, which involved taking them to bits and putting in new parts. The operation took two whole days, and I felt I was now a real engineer. But, as I was covered from head to toe in oil and grease I was a little concerned in case I had to see a patient.

Part of the diesel mechanic's responsibility was to look after the Ferguson tractors of which there were three. They may have been wonderful machines for farming in the hills of Scotland, but they were totally unsuited to the Antarctic terrain. They were equipped with tracks like a tank to give some grip on the snow surface, and it took quite a bit of skill to drive them and prevent them from bogging down. When the temperature began to fall, it became progressively more difficult to start them because the battery ceased to function when it was very cold. We hit on the idea of keeping the batteries in the warm generator shed, parking the tractors close by a ventilation shaft above, and passing a long lead to connect the battery to the tractor above. That worked very well. However, if the tractor stalled when driven away, it could not be started again; unless a tow could be organised, it would have had to be left till the following spring! When Jock and I went out to the wilds in early spring to try to recover such a tractor, we found that the bucket of pure anti-freeze we had brought with us had frozen to a solid block. Also the oil was so thick that it would not pour. We eventually solved the problem by taking with us a couple of primus stoves to thaw the anti-freeze and thin down the oil together with a battery in a heated box. Even these measures were not sufficient till we produced a couple of capsules of ether to start the engine before going over to aviation fuel. We only had a few ampoules of ether, and when that was finished, we moved on to anaesthetic ether. I was glad to unload some of the anaesthetic ether because it was so inflammable and the wood of the hut was so dry that I was hesitant to consider its use in anything other than the direst emergency. It was thus quite a thought to take a tractor out in winter. One had to be very skilled and careful when driving it in case it stalled. Nowadays, skidoos and other forms of vehicle have, of course, solved the problem.

Chapter 9

Antarctic Doctor

Mercifully, I did not have to use the operating table I had so carefully constructed. At first I was a bit disappointed, but as time passed I was more and more glad not to have many serious medical problems to solve. One problem was, however, the auroral observer who spent his nights sticking his head out of the "back door" in the roof in the freezing Antarctic night to make measurements of the various manifestations of the Aurora Australis and then back into the hot dry atmosphere of the hut. After a few months his nose started to bleed one night, and it did not respond to the usual measures. The bleeding was fairly torrential. I began to get worried at the extent of blood loss, so I decided to pack the nose. The problem was that when I removed the pack a few hours later, it just started to bleed again.

I repeated the packing and left it for twenty-four hours on two further occasions. But that did not stop the bleeding. I had found that although I thought I had the medical equipment of a battleship, I did not have a cautery, which seemed the only possible answer. Jock and I had a consultation, and he suggested that if he got the element used to ignite the ether to start the tractors, he could make a cautery. Eventually, the instrument was produced. By experiment we found that it needed two heavy-duty, twelve-volt batteries to make it hot enough, but there were no half measures. It either remained mildly warm, or as soon as you switched it on it became red hot. I suggested that we keep the batteries outside the surgery in case they frightened the patient and that the switch should be thrown at the command, "contact" and switched off immediately after. I duly removed the pack, put the cautery in place, and shouted, "Contact". Smoke belched from the nose, and there was a smell of burning similar to that when a horse is being shod. There was also a yell from the patient, but when the cautery was withdrawn the bleeding had stopped – and it remained so for the rest of the year. I was thankful that the nose did not fall off. The only explanation I could offer for the cause was that the continual gymnastics of the blood vessels in the nose, as they were repeatedly exposed to the extremes of temperature and humidity when the head was stuck out and then withdrawn, was such as to cause the vessels to enlarge and become friable.

As you might imagine I was also number two auroral observer. In addition to the measurements and descriptions made of the auroral forms, we had what was known as an all-sky camera. This was a cine camera held within a heated box and mounted on a tower built of dexion so that it pointed down to a convex mirror. The convex mirror took in the whole sky all around the horizon. A remote switch in the roof space of the hut, where the observers sat, allowed bursts of filming to take place from time to time. There was also a darkroom where the film could be processed and stored. This darkroom was also extensively used by other members since we all had cameras, and photography was practically the only hobby which was universally adopted. Like many of the others, I had little idea of photography when I arrived but soon learned. There is always a know-all in any group, and we had one too. When I rushed down for my camera because there had appeared a red aurora which is very rare, he said, "Don't bother with the camera. It is not possible to photograph a red aurora." I suddenly became very angry, grabbed my camera, and rushed outside. I screwed it to a tripod, turned it towards the sky, put my finger on the button, and kept it pressed for about fifteen minutes till it froze to the metal.

When I developed the film a few days later, I was delighted to see the red aurora but was a bit disappointed to see a couple of white marks on the film. Closer inspection, however, revealed that these were not artefacts but star movements or rather earth movements against the stars near the pole. If you looked at the heavens in the polar night and noted the position of the Milky Way and then looked again about half an hour later, it appeared to have moved round about 90 degrees. It was this effect that I had picked up on my film, and I was quite delighted to explain it to our by-this-time silent know-all.

By the beginning of March, we had settled into a more or less repetitive routine, for that is what happens on a static Antarctic base. There was the balloon launch first thing in the morning, "met. obs." every hour, the various scientific disciplines tending their projects, the gash, and the weekend dinner and film show. We were not set up to travel. That was a pity, for there was nothing new to talk about, and the same faces were there day in and day out. I was in a better position with all my number two jobs, but I had no primary responsibility in any of these areas and could be involved to the extent I chose.

As far as patients were concerned, they were few and far between though I had a few from time to time. I did have a couple of dental problems, and I performed an extraction. I had been taught how to do this by the head dentist in the Army at Millbank before I left. In those days, it was not unusual to clear the whole mouth of teeth, and after a bit of practice and instruction I cleared a couple of mouths. Nowadays that would be considered to be an act of extreme vandalism. I think it was one of Jock's teeth that I extracted. Fortunately it was in the upper jaw, for I was quite good at dental anaesthesia of the upper jaw but never very good at the lower jaw. The whole base was agog when I did this. It was not easy, for it had a long root, and the movement is one of pushing upwards and getting movement by shoulder rather than wrist movement. If you twist, you are likely to sheer off the root and that is a real disaster. Fortunately, albeit after a couple of rests, the tooth was cleanly extracted. Norman Hedderley rushed up the stairs and placed a glass of Navy rum on the table for the patient. But before he could pick it up I reached it and swallowed it with an expression of "my need is yet greater than thine".

Chapter 10

Research and the approach of Winter

By this time, my physiological experiment was established and appeared to be running reasonably well. I was kept quite busy with this initially. The first thing I had to do was to recruit four subjects. I considered this on the way down on the ship, but it took time to know the subjects. I hoped to find not only a representative sample but those who would stay the course. I chatted up Mike Sheret and Gordon Artz, two base scientists. I added to them Norman Hedderley who, as the general duties explorer, would be required to spend a fair bit of his time outside. For the fourth, I recruited John Smith who was doing a second year as the link man from the Royal Society years. John was a meteorologist, but he also made measurements of the ozone layer (which did not have a hole in it at that time) from a special hut adjacent to the main hut. This was a small hut mounted on skis so that it could be moved by tractor after a blizzard to keep it on the surface. My four subjects were well chosen, and they stayed the course, though this required much tact and diplomacy during the dark, depressing days of winter. They had to wear the temperature-sensitive vest for twenty-four hours in rotation once a month to provide a measure of the sub-clothing temperature. They also had to put up with me following them around taking measurements of the environmental temperature every fifteen minutes wherever they were. I also had to note their activity at the same time. While they may have attempted to appear more active at first during these observations, they soon settled down. I think I was able to obtain a true picture of their activity pattern together with a detailed picture of their environments minute by minute. Like all data collections over a long period, it was not easy to sustain the effort and enthusiasm of either the subjects or the experimenter over the whole period. But as a team we did quite well.

I had taken a load of books with me with a view to studying for my primary fellowship exam in surgery. I felt I would really be ahead of the pack if I could return from National Service and the Antarctic and sit the exam at the next diet. In later years I suggested this to many young men going south as an inducement to Antarctic service. This always gave me a feeling of guilt since I have to confess that I only got as far as a detailed study of one muscle – trapezius. I do not know why I started with trapezius, and at the moment, I still remember that it has something to do with the function of the shoulder but I remember little else. Perhaps if I had chosen a more interesting aspect of medical science, I could have got started more readily.

The temperature was dropping now, the nights were creeping in, and the blizzards were becoming more frequent. We thus looked out our Mukluks, put on an extra jersey and a second or a third pair of gloves, and strove to complete our preparations for winter. There were dumps of food and other stores scattered well away from the hut, and they were lying low to prevent drifting snow from burying them too deep. These had to be dug out before winter set in, re-sited, and marked so that they could be identified when it was dark. There were several dumps since we had food for two years in case the relief ship did not get in or the hut was destroyed by some accident such as fire. It took several days to complete this task. We also took the opportunity to bring as much food as possible into the hut and store it in the roof space. The job I did not like was digging out the coal. It lay in a large dump and the coal bags were all stuck together. It was very sore on the hands to claw it out. We had a large coal bunker and went through a lot of coal, for the cooking stove was really massive, and there was a stove in each of the bunk rooms. All of these were in operation twenty-four hours of the day. The sacks of coal, when dug out, had to be transported to the main hut, opened, and emptied down a shaft. It was horrible, heavy, dirty, and backbreaking work. I kept thinking of the descriptions of coaling a battleship, which I had read about in naval stories. In addition to these tasks, we had to find the dumps of chimney and aerial extensions and ensure that they were readily available. Thus there was no shortage of work in preparing for winter, particularly since each day was now becoming shorter.

The evenings spent indoors were becoming longer. As outside activity declined so did our appetites, and we began to have some difficulty sleeping. Aside from photography, there was not much to do in the evenings. The advent of the personal computer has made an enormous contribution to the well-being of personnel during Antarctic winters, but they were not available until many years later. One blessing was that we had a record player which David Limbert brought down and made generally available. Also, there was a small collection of good-quality discs. My favourite at that time was Beethoven's sixth symphony, and I can still hum almost the whole thing so often did I play it during the winter. The other disc which was very popular with me was a record of, *The Importance of Being Ernest*, with Dame Edith Evans as Lady Bracknell. I think one of its real attractions was that it allowed one to listen to new voices. To this day I can see the lounge at Halley Bay in my mind's eye every time I see a performance of *The Importance of Being Ernest*, and I can quote it almost verbatim and by the yard.

I also started to look around for something which I could do inside. So I spoke to the chief scientist, Mick Blackwell, and he suggested that I may like to help analyse the geomagnetic charts. So I became geomagnetist number five or six. The horizontal and vertical geomagnetic forces were continuously measured in a special hut adjacent to the base. The instruments were mounted on strong brick pillars, and special protective clothing was worn when the charts were changed every twenty-four hours. Nothing magnetic was allowed near the hut, and access was only allowed to the chosen few. I was taken to see these recorders on one occasion only and considered it a great privilege – almost like an audience with the Dalai Lama. The charts were photographic and were developed in batches. What was required was to work out the mean deviation up or down from a base line. A planimeter was used. This was a piece of plastic which had a calibrated scale. It was laid over the chart and a mean deviation was determined, a bit at a time, so that the hourly fluctuations could be assessed. These would then be analysed at a later date in relation to other geophysical phenomena such as auroral, ionospheric, and solar activity. If there was a lot of activity, it took ages to analyse a chart, but if there was not much, it could be done quite quickly.

I am sure that, nowadays, one would just feed the chart into a recorder or computer and the answer would come out at the other end in a matter of seconds. In any event, it took me hours upon hours to analyse one batch of charts – often working till three in the morning in the depth of winter when there was not much else to do. When I think of the effort, it reminds me of a conversation I had with Ray Adie, who was then deputy director of the British Antarctic Survey. He had spent his life as a geographer surveying and mapping the Antarctic coastline, often in dangerous and most uncomfortable conditions. Towards the end of his professional life, the Twin Otter aircraft were introduced to the Antarctic, and what had taken him a whole season to achieve could be accomplished in a couple of days by aerial photography. He did not seem unduly phased by this – probably because he had enjoyed the Antarctic experience and the company of like-minded individuals so much. In any event, I was glad to analyse the charts and have the opportunity to learn something of a scientific discipline – a discipline which was completely new to me and was likely to remain so considering the pressures of professional life on young people at home. In these days, not much time could be spared outside one's professional training in medicine for other activities, especially if one wished to make the grade in one of the major medical specialities.

Winter was the time when appetites really deteriorated, and we began to get a bit sick of dehydrated and tinned food. The sheep we had brought down from Stanley had been consumed long ago. Even on party nights there was little to stimulate the appetite even though the quality of the tinned and dehydrated food we had was of a very high standard. The one item which we all looked forward to was tinned fruit – specially raspberries on my part – but these were rationed to about once a week. At the end of the year, we discovered the cook was very proud to have been so careful with the rations and that he was able to return boxes upon boxes of tinned fruit. He may have thought that he would be recommended for the Polar Medal by a grateful administration, but he could have been seriously injured if we had discovered this earlier rather than just as we were leaving to go home! It has often been said that one of the worse jobs on a polar expedition is cooking because the cook comes in for most criticism in winter. George recognised this and created a cooking roster where each of us took a turn of cooking for a day each week during winter. We soon found that our best culinary efforts were not greatly appreciated. Indeed, one polar medical researcher made scientific measurements of stress in the Antarctic and showed that in fact of all the activities the most stressful was cooking!

We were fortunate in having a highly qualified cook from the Army Catering Corps, and he could certainly turn out some fantastic creations at times. Christmas Day and Midwinter Day spreads were magnificent to behold, as were birthdays. We all became a bit peculiar during the winter, however, and it affected us in different ways. Charlie, the cook, for example, decided that he was going to bake breakfast rolls for the next year's expedition. I had already dug out an ice cave alongside what had been the original back door, and this gave him a deep freeze of great proportions. It had to be extended, however, to accommodate the year's supply of breakfast rolls which he did produce. He also used this freezer to cause jellies to set more quickly, but it was an unpleasant experience to bite down on the spicules of ice which often formed during these culinary manoeuvres.

Jock and I used to experiment with our own cooking during the night because insomnia was another winter problem. He taught me to make a very good curry from a tin of beef, which was added to a saucepan in which dehydrated onions had been fried with curry powder. It was especially good when served with our patent brand of mango chutney. This was a mixture of apricot jam with Lea and Perrins sauce. We all had our own special ways of trying to ingratiate ourselves with our fellows with culinary surprises. One thing which I learned from Rainer Goldsmith, who had been physiologist to the Trans-Antarctic expedition advance party, was that a good squeeze of chlorophyll toothpaste gave dehydrated peas a lovely green colour and a deliciously minty flavour. He was right.

We were all supposed to congregate in the lounge after dinner and bond with each other to form a happy team, but this never really happened. Either individually or in groups we congregated in spaces dug out under the eves or in offices. In my surgery, Gordon Artz, Jock, and I used to meet quite often and just chat or do our own thing. This could be reading or darning socks, but the picture I most remember was the use of the sewing machine to make the flag for little Scotland. The radio operator, Dennis Savins, hardly ever left the radio shack from the time we arrived till we left, for he was an obsessive radio ham. There was a ventilating shaft from his shack to my surgery above, so we used to hear him making contact with the hams all over the world, telling them what hell it was living in the centre of an ice shelf in the home of the blizzard – not mentioning that he was in his very cosy little room – and reading out the "met obs" for the day. His call sign was Denmark, England, Nancy, Nancy, Italy, Spain. As can be well imagined that was a cause of some ribald comment, so it was hurriedly changed to Denmark, England, Norway, Norway, Italy Spain!

Dennis had an important job because he was our only contact with the outside world. The communication medium was Morse code, but there was so much interference that poor Dennis often had real trouble getting his reports away. In addition to the daily meteorological transmissions, each department had to send a monthly report to Cambridge on progress or problems, and we were each allowed to send one hundred words home to our families each month. This seemed a pretty niggardly allowance at first, but after about the second or third month there seemed little new to say, and it was sometimes even difficult to compose one hundred words. Nowadays with satellite communications and computers, e-mail, and fax machines one can keep in touch with home all the time. That is not necessarily an advantage because there is not much you can do if there is a problem at home in winter since you cannot get back.

The scientists and met men used their offices to work on their observations and to socialise, while Mike Sheret spent his evenings observing the aurora through the roof. The gash hands finished their duties and had their allocated bath. The duty met men were watching the weather recorders in their offices. All in all only George Lush and the cook socialised in the lounge. We did, however, all come together on Saturday nights in our good suits after the big scrub out, as was the British tradition. That was important. Every now and again we would have a big party when George produced a stone jar of Navy rum. After midwinter, however, even parties did not develop very often.

I have been aware of a kind of lethargy and mild depression in the darkness of winter even at home in Scotland, and I always feel much brighter after the winter solstice in December. This gets worse the further north you go. There is a medical condition called melancholia orcadiensis found in the Orkney Islands, which is much worse in winter. Modern medicine suggests that this is related to the secretion of melatonin from the pineal body stimulated and regulated by light passing through the eyes. We researched this many years later in Halley though I always felt that it was not necessary to invoke a hormone to account for a feeling of depression during the Antarctic winter. I had all my little jobs to keep me amused – the launching of the balloon in the morning, my physiology experiment, the servicing of the generators and the tractors, the preparations for the penguin embryo collection together with the analysis of the geomagnetic charts in the evenings. In the afternoons, if nothing else was happening, I would creep into the lounge – silent and usually deserted in winter – and play Beethoven's Sixth Symphony or listen to *The Importance of Being Ernest*.

Chapter 11

In Search of Penguin Embryos

With the approach of winter my biological project began to assume some urgency, and I did not want to let Sir Raymond Priestley down. I had given it some thought from time to time since we arrived, but the more I thought about it the more I realized that I had little idea of how I was going to achieve the collection of a timed series of emperor penguin embryos. At that time I had not read Cherry-Garrard's great book, *The Worst Journey in the World*, and I expect I may have been put off if I had. The privations suffered by the three men who made the 70-mile winter journey to the rookery at Cape Crozier was mind-boggling; they were lucky to escape with their lives. By the time they arrived at the cliffs above Cape Crozier in darkness, extreme cold, and a blizzard much of their equipment had been lost or damaged. They then had to abseil down the cliffs and climb back up. After the second attempt their tent was lost, and they were in a desperate state. The journey ranks as one of the classic stories of Antarctic exploration and heroism. Yet they only managed to return with three emperor penguin embryos, and I was expected to produce a precisely timed series of embryos at twelve-hour intervals for ten days!

Only Cherry-Garrard returned alive from the Antarctic. Britain was at war with Germany by that time. In addition, the professor at the Natural History Museum, who shared Dr Wilson's burning interest in the embryology of the emperor penguin, had died. No one else seemed at all interested in emperor penguins. After the suffering endured in collecting the embryos and the loss of his comrades that must have been a real and deep disappointment for Cherry-Garrard. He went off to war. The embryos were taken over by another professor. However, he also died a short time later, and the embryos passed into obscurity.

I had several long discussions with George Lush, and I soon came to realize how truly invaluable he was to us. He decided that since the penguins laid their eggs in June — the coldest and darkest month of the year – the only way for me to achieve the project was to go and live at Emperor Bay. This was easier said than done, and I did not really know where to start. George, however, set to and constructed a caboose from a Ferguson tractor packing case, which he insulated and mounted securely on a Maudheim sledge – the type of large sledge used to transport stores from the ship to the base. It was just big enough to build in two bunk beds of dexion – one on top of the other. Between the end of the bunks and the end of the box he fashioned a broad shelf upon which were mounted two primus stoves, and beneath the shelf there was room for clothing and other stores. Beside the lower bunk was a second small shelf, and this was the shelf where the eggs would be dissected to recover the embryos. There was even an operating light above it. It was agreed that I could also have a small mobile diesel electric generator capable of producing seven kilowatts of power, and there was a one-kilowatt electric radiator inside. So well was the box insulated that that was all that was necessary to keep the caboose reasonably comfortable. There was also a light outside so that we could find it in the dark. In the event, the caboose was very comfortable in the minus forties of temperature, but there was a thermal gradient so that the temperature close to the ground could be just above freezing, and near the roof it was +70 or even 80 degrees Fahrenheit. Within the caboose, clothing worn tended to be full Antarctic gear to the waist and nothing above it.

In a winter blizzard, there was always the possibility of the sea

61

ice breaking up as we had seen happen in the summer during the unloading of the ship. After some discussion it was decided that the caboose would be sited on the cliff overlooking Emperor Bay (but not too close to the edge) rather than on the sea ice where the penguins would be. Emperor Bay was about 4 kilometres from Halley Bay and looked very similar. It was a bit like a creek with ice cliffs on each side of the sea ice and a ramp from the sea ice which led up to the ice shelf 200 feet or so above.

While there was still daylight and we could still start the tractors without too much difficulty, we towed the caboose down to Emperor Bay and sited it on the cliff above. It was a matter of judgement – or possibly of luck – to determine how close to the edge of the cliff to place it, and we parked it so that the rear faced the prevailing wind. A few years later, Emperor Bay and the adjacent cliffs disappeared altogether during a blizzard when the area broke off the ice shelf and became a large iceberg. If that had happened during our tenure, we may also have had a " Worst Journey in the World" and proceeded towards home long before we were due to leave!!

The next thing to do was to pull down the Enfield generator which was also mounted on a Maudheim sledge, and we started it and ran it for a while. Since our lives could depend on the function of this generator, Jock and I subjected it to a very thorough service. It would have to run continuously for up to two months, for if we stopped it we may not be able to start it again. We also took down half a dozen forty-gallon drums of fuel, and we had our own little food dump alongside the sledge. Altogether it looked reasonably comfortable. I developed a passion for buttered asparagus tips during the passage home, though I never liked asparagus before that time. Charlie had given us several cases of asparagus, so we used them to shore up weak parts of the installation against the weather. I often think of that when I have asparagus as a treat in a restaurant in more salubrious surroundings. The reason for my change of view on asparagus was that on the voyage home, the ship's cook was a chef from the Savoy in London and he had signed on to have a look at the Deep South. When he produced asparagus, the ship's officers counted the spears on each plate and were furious if one of them got an extra piece.

When I thought the project through, it had become clear that it really was a two-man job. Two are always better than one when a difficult project is considered. I approached Mike Sheret, the auroral observer – you will recall that I was also auroral observer number two – and I was delighted that he agreed to come. I was very grateful particularly since the period around midwinter is the time when the aurora is most active. When we discussed things, we realized that we could share the biological and auroral work between us since they both required twenty-four-hour presence. I could not know when the timing of an embryo would begin, and Mike may need a shout if there was a particularly fine display in the middle of the twenty-four-hour night. A fringe benefit of this was that since one of us had to be around, there would be little argument about who got the hot bunk and who got the cold.

We discussed this with George and once again he rose to the occasion by building a porch on to the front of the caboose with a sliding roof which could act as the auroral observatory. The porch also added additional protection during bad weather. Mike was also a Scot. He hailed from Kirkcaldy. We therefore called our mini-base at Emperor Bay "Little Scotland". In order to underline this, we felt we should have a flag, particularly when we were in residence, and that it should be the lion rampant. An old pillow case was produced, and we stained it yellow with acriflavine emulsion from the surgery. I then found I had a scarlet Army PT shirt, and after cutting out the shape of the rampant lion we spent a few happy early winter evenings preparing the flag. The flag flew proudly over the door of Little Scotland during our tenure of the establishment.

During the month of June when we would be away from the main base, it was dark for twenty-four hours of the day, and the weather can be very bad. I still had to provide medical cover for the base, and although there was not much sickness, some problem may arise when I was away and out of communication with the base. Equally, since the ice shelf is totally featureless, one usually needed a compass to find Emperor Bay during the summer. How could we find Little Scotland in the dark and particularly in white-out blizzard conditions even if we could see a compass? In a blizzard you are lucky to see more than a few yards ahead, and in the Antarctic night nothing at all. If the caboose was missed, the next stop was a fall of 200 feet to the sea ice below, if you went in one direction, and nothing if you went in the other!

The solution we arrived at was to lay down a series of bamboo canes at fifty or a hundred yards distance from each other from the main base to Emperor Bay. The problem with this was that it was now getting well towards winter, and a tractor was needed to carry the canes. Rather than risking stalling the tractor, we drove it from the base to the caboose throwing off the bamboos at appropriate intervals. This was accomplished without incident, and the tractor returned safely to the main base. We erected the canes next day on foot. Thereafter we got a ball of string and tied it between the bamboos so that we could always feel our way along. This may have seemed excessive, but I was very glad of that string on several occasions when I was disorientated in dark, blizzard conditions and could not see where the next or the previous bamboo was. We were short of a couple of bamboos, so there was about a hundred yards from the end of the bamboo chain to the caboose, which was not covered. We considered what we had to be adequate and were pleased with our preparations. That was great, but it did not solve the communication problem.

I do not remember where it came from, but someone produced an army field telephone and a great coil of telephone wire. We then attached the telephone wire to the bamboos with the string and joined a receiver to each end – the main base end was in the met office which was manned twenty-four hours per day. The other end was in the caboose beside the operating shelf for the egg dissections. To my surprise, this arrangement worked perfectly right away and remained functional for the whole period of our residence at Emperor Bay. We now had a line to follow between the two huts, which would allow us to find our way in the worst weather and in the total darkness of winter, and we could also communicate both ways. The final task was to establish a line of bamboos from the headland down to the sea ice and join them together with string so that we could find our way up and down in bad conditions with safety. We were now ready to begin our work and were pretty proud of the preparations we had made, which were the result of real team effort among base members. But undoubtedly it would not have been possible without the near genius and construction ability of the ex-bosun, George Lush. It was good for the base to have a deviation from the routine, and they all took a real interest in what we were trying to do. It was the end of April by the time our preparations were completed and with winter fast approaching. But there was no sign of a penguin! We ceremoniously opened the satellite base of Little Scotland at Emperor Bay, however. At the end of the year when the post office was established at Halley Bay we carried a bunch of letters by sledge from Halley Bay to Little Scotland and achieved the postmaster's attestation.

Tottan heading South into pancake ice after crossing the Antarctic circle.

Tottan arriving at Halley Bay and nudging sea ice to prepare a berth for herself. Photographer, LW Barclay, 1958. Reproduced courtesy of NERC-BAS. British Antarctic Survey Archives Service. Ref. AD6/19/X/25/52.

Ferguson tractors on sea ice preparing to unload Tottan now anchored to ice.

Tottan anchored to slope leading to ice shelf after the sea ice had dramatically broken up and gone to sea. Photographer LW Barclay, 1958. Reproduced courtesy of NERC-BAS. British Antarctic Survey Archives Service. Ref. AD6/19/X/25/51

Hitching a lift over featureless ice shelf to the base camp. The Ferguson tractor pulls two Maudheim sledges.

First sight of Halley Bay station, 1958. Not much to see as it is largely buried by drifting snow or embedded in the ice shelf.

The 'front door'. The boxing leads to a shaft and the actual entrance to the hut is some thirty feet below. Photographer, Wm Freeland.

The 'back door'. This is a series of packing cases mounted on top of each other on the apex of the roof. Mike Sheret is peeping out. The chimneys which were extended after each blizzard are also seen.

Pre-prandial drinks in the cosy bar on a Saturday night. L to R Gordon Artz, Jock Whitehall, Jim Mace, David Limbert, Norman Hedderley and George Lush.

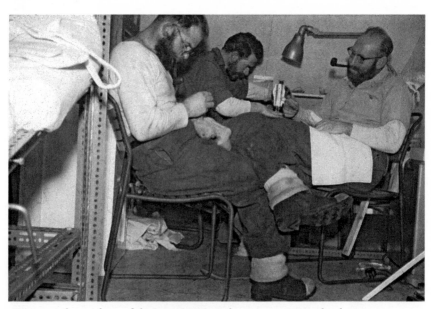

Contented members of the 'sewing B' in the surgery. Note the dexion operating table on the left. Jock Whitehall is darning socks, Norman Hedderley using the sewing machine and Gordon Artz is writing a letter.

Launching a weather balloon in a modest storm.

Recovering fuel drums after a winter blizzard using flood lights. Photographer, DF Patuck, 1976. Reproduced courtesy of NERC-BAS. British Antarctic Survey Archives Service. Ref. AD6/193/D100.

Chapter 12

Emperor Bay

The days became progressively shorter as winter approached until 4 May when the sun finally set for the last time for three months. It was an odd sensation, and it was accompanied by a kind of silence, which was somehow ominous. It did not bother us too much at the time, but as winter progressed one began to wonder whether we would ever see daylight again. After that we only ventured outside when necessary and George Lush had done such a good job of preparing for winter that it was not necessary, except for "met obs", launching balloons, and extending the chimneys and aerials after blizzards. It was not totally dark for the twenty-four hours, for a rim of red just peeped above the horizon for some time at midday, and then there was a kind of glow on the horizon which lasted for an hour or so. I went down to Emperor Bay about once a week to check on Little Scotland, to test the communications, and to look for penguins. Although the caboose stood up well to the elements, the communications continued to work, and the generator started with ease, there was no sign of a single penguin. It was very good for me to make these trips, for it got me out of the main hut for a purpose while the others had no excuse to go anywhere.

I continued to make my weekly visits to Emperor Bay and was getting quite worried by the continued absence of penguins. All remained deathly silent until one day, as the midday glow appeared above the horizon, I was aware of a great noise coming from the sea ice. When I got to the bluff overlooking the bay I met the most remarkable sight. There was a great column of emperor penguins marching in pairs and going right back to the horizon. The whole bay was rapidly filling with penguins. The noise was terrific as they all chattered away excitedly while taking up their new winter quarters. There appeared to be thousands of penguins. In previous years, it had been estimated that there were about eight or ten thousand eventually. It was obvious that the breeding season was upon us. With a measure of relief and some excitement, I repaired urgently to the base and alerted Michael. We packed our bags and proceeded to take up residence in Little Scotland.

We raised the standard on arrival and started the generator. It was a relief to find that it started, for the temperature was −43 degrees Centigrade and it was covered with rime. It kept going without stopping for the next six weeks, and this says much for the service it had received from Jock. We unpacked our kit and found that the primus stoves worked well immediately, so we made tea. This also meant that we had to melt some snow, and that took ages, for nothing is easy in the Antarctic. You would be surprised how much snow you have to melt to make a cup of tea. It did, however, appear that our conditions during the attempted collection of the embryos were going to be much more comfortable than Cherry-Garrard described for his winter journey with Dr Wilson and Lieutenant Bowers. We had the benefit of time to prepare, and we had the industry and ingenuity of George Lush; that was to count for a good deal.

After our tea we wandered down to the rookery to have a look and to consider how we would set about our task. Fortunately we did not need to abseil down to the sea ice because we had a gentle slope and were guided by bamboos joined together with string. In any event, although there was no sun, it was not pitch black at that time because there was a bright full moon, and when our eyes became used to the darkness, we could see quite well. It was more difficult when there was no moon, but we could always see what we were doing. When the wind caused drifting snow, it was much more difficult.

The penguins were still arriving. There were groups scattered all over the sea ice chattering and making a terrific noise. They were obviously trying to choose a site for the winter. As time passed they tended to group together in huddles, but that had not yet happened. A main problem was that we knew very little of the normal processes of penguin reproduction at that time since there was so much to do before we left and we had not obtained any of the relevant publications, even though there were a few available at that time. The enormity of our task did, however, dawn on us when we saw the many thousands of identical-looking penguins rushing about. We considered that it would not be easy to identify a penguin, say, precisely 6.5 days after it had laid an egg – particularly if it was dark, very cold, and blowing a gale. It seemed clear that it was necessary to select a smaller population than ten thousand, so we decided to construct a kind of corral by hammering fence posts into the ice and closing the intervals with chicken wire netting. We knew such equipment was available at the main base although we were not sure what its primary purpose was. This meant a return journey to the main base and the transport of the posts to Emperor Bay by manhaul sledge.

Neither Michael nor I was, however, a glaciologist. We had no idea how hard ice was or how difficult it would be to hammer the posts into the ice, though we remembered how long it had taken to anchor the *Tottan* to the ice. It took nearly a day to hammer a dozen posts into the ice with a sledge hammer, and they did not seem all that secure. When the chicken wire had been applied and we were ready to place a few penguins in the stockade, we found that the whole mass of penguins had moved nearly half a mile away. Although we had begun erecting the corral in the middle of the rookery, the noise and vibration of our efforts were presumably such that the rookery had moved to get away from it. We were so preoccupied with the task in hand that we had failed to notice this exodus.

The distance from the corral was obviously going to cause problems in herding a sample into it, for they were big birds, nearly 4 ½ feet high, weighing about a hundredweight, and with a mind of their own. They had great curved beaks and flippers, which it has been said could break a man's arm with a blow. Fortunately they were a bit stupid and non-aggressive, so they did us no harm. They were, however, not easy to catch. On land, they waddle awkwardly, but they can move fast when you chase them and they flop onto their bellies and toboggan along. A chase in full polar gear was not easy for us because when we became a bit breathless, we had to suck in large volumes of very cold air. This was uncomfortable, and I was a little concerned that air below -40 degrees Centigrade sucked in through the mouth rather than the nose might be dangerous if spicules of ice were to end up in the lungs. This has been reported in exercising horses in Alaska. After several hours, we had three bedraggled penguins in our corral. Defeated and a bit depressed, we retired to the caboose to consider the matter and work out our next plan of attack.

Meantime, eggs had started to appear. When the egg is laid, the penguin places it on her feet and covers it with a fold of loose lower abdominal skin to keep it warm. She then walks along on her heels in a very distinctive manner with a bulge above her feet so that it is very obvious that she had laid an egg. Jock visited us at this juncture and constructed a device which consisted of two poles with a piece of string between them. We called it the patent Whitehall bird bodge. You came up behind the penguin, hooked the string over its head, and with a twist you had caught the bird. That worked quite well, and it was possible to catch a penguin a reasonable number of times. The problem was that the penguin would often not proceed in the direction we wished and since the bird was so heavy, we sometimes had difficulty in moving it at all. It seemed that if both of us pulled really hard we would either strangle the bird or pull its head off! With the beginnings of mild panic, we once more headed back to the caboose for a cup of tea

We next remembered the coal bags which were empty after coaling the base, so we returned yet again to the main base for a supply of coal bags and a sledge. The idea was to catch the bird with the bird bodge and somehow get it into the coal bag. It was then transported to the corral on the sledge. It was very hard work and very slow, but we made progress. It was certainly not easy to get a huge penguin into a coal bag, and it was equally difficult to get it back out. But eventually we had eight or nine black and bedraggled penguins in the corral. I could not help thinking that if any of them were pregnant, they would probably abort. It would have been just our luck if they had all been male penguins. It was impossible for me to sex a penguin, but I had noticed that they seemed to go about in pairs. So while one of us was chasing and transporting a penguin, the other was keeping an eye on its partner, which we also caught and transported next. The last straw would have been if there had been gay penguins!

It was all very well to have our penguin collection in the corral, but we still had to find a way of identifying them individually. I felt that was no problem because I had seen plenty of paint at the main base and a collection of stencils for packing cases. So we trotted back yet again, secured what was necessary, and tried the experiment with confidence. Surprise, surprise, it did not work. As soon as we opened the tin of paint and stuck the brush in, the whole issue froze solid. It was a short, sharp experiment, and to say it was frustrating was mild. We were so dispirited that we decided to return to the base to see if anyone could come up with suggestions. George suggested tying labels round their necks. He also suggested that we should cut out pieces of plywood and paint numbers on them at the base, and instead of using string, we should construct loops of wire which we could attach to the labels and drop them over their heads. This took nearly a day to achieve, and we did not make too many till we saw whether the idea worked. It was with much surprise that we found that the idea did work, though it was dangerous getting the wire over the penguins' heads with the great curved, sharp beak.

We now had a collection of twenty penguins inside the corral, and although eggs were being laid indiscriminately all around us, our bunch in the corral showed not the slightest interest in reproduction. By this time the breeding season was well advanced since our efforts had taken more than two weeks. We decided to give it a bit more time but did not feel great confidence. It had become really cold, and the temperature did not rise above −40 degrees Centigrade for the whole month of June. Fortunately there were no severe blizzards, although there were several minor blows and a lot of drift, so we were only unable to venture forth on two or three occasions.

By this time the rookery had formed itself into a single massive huddle, which remained relatively quiet but did seem to be moving all the time in a shuffling sort of way. This seemed to be a kind of temperature regulation as the movement allowed them to take turns of exposing themselves to the cold edge. It may of course have been the stronger or more aggressive ones who managed to maintain a place well into the huddle and the weaker and less fortunate ones who kept finding themselves on the edge. On one occasion something caused the huddle to move several yards laterally, and I was surprised to find that they were in fact standing in a great pool of water. Thus the huddle must have generated considerable heat.

The other thing which nagged at the back of my mind was when to start the timing of the embryos since we lived on an ice shelf 200 feet above the sea ice and may not be there when an egg was laid. This exercised my mind as I wandered around the rookery, and I just could not think of an answer. It was all very depressing.

Chapter 13

The Solution

One day as I wandered disconsolately around the huddle pondering the problem, I noticed a penguin leaving the huddle and standing outside. There seemed to be rhythmic movements of its lower abdomen, and I began to wonder whether I was observing a penguin in labour. Some time later out popped the egg, which she placed rapidly on her feet and re-entered the huddle. If only I had had a label with me or the penguin had been in the corral! Some time later the performance was repeated, and it took about twenty minutes for the egg to appear. This was much the same as the first episode. It thus seemed that we could see eggs laid if we just observed the huddle closely, and we had about twenty minutes to do something about identifying the bird.

I repaired rapidly to the caboose with this information for a discussion with Mike. After much talk we remembered that we had a quantity of dexion at the main base and wondered whether we could construct a kind of cage in which we could gently incarcerate the bird after the egg was laid. Another visit to the main base and a discussion with George allowed the construction of a few cages, which were lined with more of the chicken wire. One side the chicken wire was attached only to one edge so that it would act as a door. This cage was mounted on a Nansen sledge.

This was now very much a two-man job. I set about looking for a labouring penguin. When I found one, I signalled to Mike, who pulled the sledge over as gently and quietly as possible behind the penguin and removed the cage from the sledge. This had to be done quietly, and Mike may have been some way off when he got the signal. When he arrived at the scene, Mike gently removed the cage from the sledge and placed it with the door open behind the bird. When the egg was laid, he slid the cage gently over the penguin and I stepped forward, closed the door, hung a numbered label on the door, and noted the time. It did not always work, however, because if we made a noise or were too slow, the bird would take off for the huddle rapidly, sometimes even abandoning the egg. After a couple of successes, however, we reckoned that we had cracked the technique. So we let the other poor souls out of the corral – none of them had laid an egg in any case – and returned to our caboose in high spirits to celebrate. I do not think we had a bottle with us, so we probably just had a cup of tea and one of Charlie's morning rolls with butter and jam.

Since the first egg would be harvested in twelve hours, arrangements had to be made for the recovery of the embryo. The egg was of considerable size, and it was mounted on a lump of plasticine to keep it steady while the dissection was carried out. The plasticine was laid on the little shelf in the caboose constructed for that purpose and fitted with a light above it. I had to cut a square out of the top very carefully with a hacksaw and gently reflect it back. The shell was very thick, and this took quite a long time, for there must be no damage to the contents. The embryo was a small, white plaque sitting on top of the yolk, so you had to go down through the white albumen and dissect it off without bursting the yolk. If you burst the yolk, the whole field was obscured and you were liable to lose the embryo in the mess. Fortunately, that happened only once, but it caused much fury and gnashing of teeth for it was near the end of the collection and laying had all but stopped by that time. When the embryo was removed, it was placed in a small bottle of Bouin's solution and carefully labelled.

Before the dissection took place, the egg had to be harvested and transported back to the caboose. Since the time was set, the recovery of the egg had to take place quickly no matter what the weather conditions were like. In the main, the weather was reasonably stable, but eggs had to be recovered in blizzards on one or two occasions. At these times

I was very glad that I was able to feel my way down along the string which joined the bamboo poles together. Before leaving the caboose, I placed a sea-boot stocking next to my skin with the top protruding at the neck. When I had recovered the egg, I manoeuvred it into the stocking and the sub-clothing warmth and journeyed back up the cliff to the caboose. This effectively prevented damage to the egg from the cold or trauma

This was often achieved in pitch blackness and blizzard conditions over very uneven terrain, so it could be quite hazardous. Visibility was so poor on the cliff that it would have been virtually impossible if we had not had the bamboo poles joined with string to guide us to the sea ice. Visibility was better on the sea ice because there was less snow there to drift. I was always aware of the sudden break-up of the sea ice during the unloading of the ship, and I knew that if that had happened there was no Captain Jacobsen to come to my aid. On one occasion, I got a real fright because as I was proceeding up the slope there were loud noises and cracks coming from beneath the ice, and I thought the whole thing was breaking up. As it was midwinter I thought it unlikely that the ice was about to break up, but I wondered whether the cliff was coming adrift. I had no idea what was happening. I had just been reading about leopard seals and killer whales and the story of a shipwrecked mariner sitting adrift on an ice floe with a leopard seal standing by waiting for him to go to sleep before attacking. My imagination immediately made me think that one or a group of such creatures was trying to break through in search of its supper. I made the top of the slope in record time that day.

By the time we had convinced ourselves that the task was virtually impossible the redoubtable George Lush built an incubator at the main base and invited us to place some eggs in it. I did not know what temperature to set it at, and I was not sure that it would work, but I placed a few eggs in it. I went up to harvest the first embryo at the base and had quite an audience around me to observe the procedure. As I bent down closely to the egg, I was just removing the flap of shell when the whole thing blew up with a really loud bang. The egg had gone bad, and what was worse than the fright the explosion gave us, we were covered with its most foul contents. The smell of hydrogen sulphide remained on us for several days! That was the last of George's incubated eggs that I had the courage to open. Fortunately, our cages were shown to work about the same time.

If we were both around, we usually went down together for safety and company and also because much that had to be done was a two-man job – particularly the detection of a laying bird and its incarceration. We were not always both available, for the aurora also had to be observed, and both the auroral displays and the timing of the recovery of the embryos could take place at awkward times. It was just as well that our duties were staggered, for the sleeping arrangements were subject to the temperature gradient within the hut. The temperature in the space of the lower bunk was not much above freezing while that in the space of the upper bunk was between 70 and 80 degrees Fahrenheit. It was difficult to determine which space was preferable, but that did not matter too much as it was not often that we both wished to sleep at the same time. The best technique was for one to start in the upper bunk and then slip down below for a while after waking in a muck sweat. This would almost certainly have created problems if both of us wanted to sleep at the same time.

This was a very busy period, for we were approaching the end of the laying period and labouring birds were becoming more and more difficult to find. We also had to procure more cages. Fortunately the weather still held, for a real blizzard would have destroyed the whole process. We were in fact becoming a bit too confident because the technique was so successful. When you get carried away with your own brilliance, disaster often strikes to bring you back to earth and to indicate that you are in the hands of the Gods and not brilliant at all. And so it was that when I wandered down to harvest the four-day specimen, I was horrified to find that the egg had been rejected by its mother and lay in a frozen state in a corner of the cage. I hoped that this was an unusual occurrence, but when it happened with the four-and-a-half-day embryo, it was obviously something more serious.

At this time someone found a report by Bernard Stonehouse about penguins at the bottom of a filing cabinet. We found to our horror that at three days after laying, the female transfers the egg to her male partner and the male then completes the incubation while the female goes off fishing. She may, of course, need to walk for several hundred miles to find access to the sea, so it is not much fun. She finally swims back sleek and full of nutrients to feed the young and allow the male to go off. This whole process may take several weeks or even months, and the timing of her return – and thus the survival of the young – depends upon when the sea ice breaks up to allow a passage. After all this time, she is able to return to her offspring for which she now shows much more motherly affection! In 1959, the sea ice was in fact late in breaking up and mortality in the chicks was high. This in fact resulted in some fierce fights. The desire for parenthood was such that if there was considerable mortality among the chicks and one was seen wandering about, fierce attempts to adopt it often resulted in the death of yet another chick!

It may be that our disaster was due to us forgetting the transfer – but it is equally likely that it was due to sheer ignorance of the process! In any event, it seemed clear that if we were going to get over this problem, we would need to incarcerate the male with his partner. Fortunately, we had had ample opportunity to observe the behaviour of these birds while we attended their labour and sought new birds in labour. When the female goes into labour, she emerges from the huddle and proceeds to lay her egg. Meanwhile in an almost human way a second bird emerges, and this is presumably the male. He usually paces up and down, just like an anxious father outside a maternity ward. After the birth of the egg they both return to the huddle. Occasionally, if the affair becomes a bit protracted, he will bend his head down to have a look to see if anything can be seen. On one occasion, when it was a very cold day, the father kept rushing back to the huddle for a heat and then came running back to see how things were going. There was little doubt in our minds that we were in a position to identify the father. This was now more like a three-man job because we had to keep an eye on the father and, after the female had been incarcerated, capture him before he could disappear into the anonymity of the huddle. We were very determined by this time and used every effort, including the Whitehall bird bodge, since laying birds were few and far between. Four days after the incarceration we released the bird which did not have the egg, and it disappeared into the wide blue yonder. The fact that the remaining bird on every occasion continued with the incubation until the allotted time proved that we had at last got it right.

By these means we finally managed to obtain the required precisely timed twenty embryos, but I think the last one may have been from the last egg to be laid that year! The rookery had become quite silent despite the presence of several thousand birds. They were all in one giant huddle, heads well down; there was only a slight rustling as they moved about within the huddle. Presumably the huddle consisted almost entirely of males since the females would have gone off fishing. It could, of course, be that the males who did not have an egg to incubate would also have departed. Laying eggs was not entirely without its obstetric problems, for there were a few dead blood-stained penguins left on the sea ice after the event. The males were quite remarkable because they did not eat for the six weeks they were left on their own, and they did have to keep warm, which would presumably take a fair bit of energy in these climes. We only lost one embryo during transportation or dissection, and the feeling of achievement was felt throughout the base – rightly so, for everyone had made some sort of contribution. It was an achievement for the whole base.

Chapter 14

Related activities at Little Scotland

We had three dexion cages, and when all the cages were occupied, Mike and I discussed the possibility of recording the birth of an egg on film. This required both light and a camera system, which would not immediately seize up in the intense cold. By this time we were gaining experience in solving impossible problems in the Antarctic environment. Mike suggested that we might try to use his all-sky camera since it was basically just a 16-millimetre cine camera and functioned within a specially heated and insulated box. If anything went wrong with this camera, Mike's research project would come to a sticky end, so it was with some trepidation that we decided to give it a try. We therefore returned to the base, removed the camera from its tower, and transported it to Little Scotland without incident. Fortunately it was still in working order. A test on the sea ice confirmed also that the set-up functioned quite effectively, but there was still the problem of light. There was a full moon at this time, and we wondered whether this would be sufficient since we were using very fast film, but it was not. That was a bit of a blow, but by this time we were used to coming up against apparently impossible problems. So we trotted back to the base to determine whether there were any suggestions.

This time it was one of the meteorologists who laughingly made the suggestion that we should try using the cloud searchlight. This was a powerful light source which was shone upwards in the polar night to determine the height of the cloud base. It required a strong energy source, and a battery would not be enough even if it would work for long enough to do the job and that was highly unlikely. We had a powerful source of energy, however, in the form of our Enfield generator, but it was at the top of the cliff, and the penguins were more than a mile away on the sea ice. Since we had achieved the embryo collection successfully, I suppose, we were on the crest of a wave and felt that we could triumph over all manner of adversities. This time a hair-brained scheme actually worked. We had no proper electrical cable, and, in any case, we needed more than a mile. However, we had a large drum of field telephone wire. We mounted the cloud searchlight on the sledge used to transport the cages, brought the telephone wire from the generator beside the caboose on the cliff down to the sea ice, and connected it to the searchlight. When it was first switched on, we expected a mighty explosion somewhere in the system, but the searchlight lit up with a powerful beam and remained lit.

Before anything else went wrong we rapidly proceeded with the filming using the tried techniques of the past few weeks. I found a bird in labour and signalled to Mike to produce the filming equipment. The next problem was that the ice was not smooth, and there were bits the size of a pebble which protruded and the cable became caught up on them requiring the sledge handler to return to the problem site to undo the snagged cable. It took ages for the equipment to arrive and every time there was a snag, we expected the light to go out as the cable ruptured. It all became very fraught and time after time the penguin had returned to the huddle with her egg long before the searchlight arrived. Eventually, however, we were fortunate enough to find a suitable subject when the searchlight was close and we got the sequence. I was worried in case the light would frighten the bird and send her scurrying off but this did not happen. We then returned the camera to the main base and were relieved to find that it still functioned properly. When we developed the film, the images were of surprisingly good quality. Since we had gone to so much trouble to get the setup to work, we cast around for something else to use it for but there was nothing else to photograph. We had, however, achieved our main objective and decided to quit while we were still ahead. The surprising thing was that the telephone wire lasted so well, did not cause the generator to explode, the caboose to burn down, or one of us to be electrocuted!

The caboose lasted well and provided us not only with shelter from both the cold and the blizzards but also with a modicum of comfort. The cooking arrangements worked well also, and we had plenty of food – possibly even the occasional tin of fruit. I still have very fond memories of the packet of kippers with which we were provided, for I have never tasted anything quite so good before or since. We took a few penguin eggs up to the main base, and when Charlie cracked one into his massive frying pan it completely filled it. They were not, however, very good; they had a strong flavour of fish. The white, however, made terrific meringues and could be used for cakes or even baked Alaska. The old explorers – including Shackleton's party after they were beset – did eat penguin eggs quite often.

Many years later at Rothera on the Antarctic Peninsula I remembered seeing the staked out dog team sleeping contentedly in the sun when an Adelie penguin came wandering by. It was an idyllic Antarctic scene. Suddenly, there was a scuffle, and all that was left of the penguin was a couple of feathers floating above where it had been. We had a pet Husky dog at Halley Bay. It had rather short legs for sledging and had been rejected by a sledging team which visited the Royal Society group. On account of its short legs, it was called Stumpy. John Smith looked after it and built it a kennel, which was sited close to one of the shafts. It used the kennel during major blizzards and seemed quite happy to remain outside in all weathers. It visited us and remained for a few days. During this time, there was a blizzard and since it did not have a kennel I decided to bed it down in the porch. That was a mistake because the heat caused the snow on its coat to melt, and it became both wet and smelly. What surprised me was that it now seemed quite small. This must have been due to the thickness of the fur and the trapping of vast quantities of the poor conductor – air.

While we were in residence at Little Scotland I actually had a medical call one night and the field telephone proved its worth. This was the man who was in charge of the hut mounted on a sledge, which contained the instrument used to measure the thickness of the ozone layer. It had to be re-sited after a blizzard to keep it on the surface. He struggled for several hours to move it in a temperature of -43 degrees Centigrade, and when he finished he began to spit blood. By the time I was called, the blizzard had returned, and I set out to see him in terrible conditions. I suppose this was with a certain amount of bravado, for I would not normally have ventured forth in such conditions. But knowing also the politics of winter, I felt I would lose much face if I did not respond to the call immediately. I felt the journey would be reasonably straightforward, for we were well used to crawling along the bamboo chain to the main base – albeit not in such foul conditions. I was well wrapped up when I left the hut. I could see nothing in the dark, and the drifting snow ensured that I could hardly see a hand in front of me. It was then that I remembered there was a gap between the hut and the beginning of the bamboo chain, for we had been short of a couple of bamboos when we laid down the chain. This had never bothered us before because we had always travelled in reasonable weather, and even in moderate drift, the gloaming or moonlight was such that you could always see the first bamboo.

I suppose the missing bamboo came to mind that night since I could see nothing at all. It was only a few yards, however, and I knew the direction very well by that time so I set off. After a little I looked back and had a mild pang of fear when I realized that I could not see the caboose. This was not normally a problem since we had a bright light on the hut which was lit, but there was no sign of it. I decided to press on but after about a hundred yards I became aware that I should certainly have crossed the link between the bamboos by that time. Another look back did not help and only made me realize that I was completely disorientated. With a mounting sense of panic I also discovered that I had left in such a hurry that I had forgotten my compass, and though I felt that I should veer to the left I was so disorientated that I could not be sure. Even if I had a compass I doubt whether I could have seen it. Fortunately the gear I had on meant that I was reasonably comfortable, so I stopped and considered what to do. After a bit of thought I realized that if I continued in my present direction and missed the bamboo chain I would head for the desolate, featureless wilderness of the ice shelf, but if I returned and missed the tiny caboose I would be likely walk over the cliff edge. I therefore decided to proceed towards the wilderness and veer to the left which

I was pretty certain was the direction of the main base and to zigzag. I did this and after about fifteen of the most terrifying minutes of my life I walked into a bamboo cane. I clung to it tightly as waves of relief passed over me. I had no idea how far along the chain it was, and I clung on to the string and wire firmly all the way to the main base. Even when I arrived at the base I had a few moments of panic since I was disorientated there and had difficulty in finding the entrance to the hut.

When I met my patient he was sitting up in the warm bunk room full of the joys, feeling fine and my examination revealed no abnormality. As I had suspected before I left Little Scotland I think he was suffering from the frosting of lungs occasionally seen in horses in winter in Alaska. It is caused when ice spicules form in the lung during mouth breathing in very cold weather. These spicules prick the lining of the lung and make it bleed. There was nothing to be done apart from providing reassurance. The patient confirmed that he had been heaving at a recalcitrant sledge in an attempt to re-site the hut mounted on it and had been mouth breathing from the exertion.

After a cup of cocoa I phoned Mike at Little Scotland and told him that I would not return that night but would come the next day if the weather moderated. I did not admit to my panic-stricken adventure since I felt that it was my own stupid fault. It did underline the fact that you cannot allow any slackness or loss of vigilance to safety in a place like the Antarctic if accidents are to be avoided – or even if you are to survive.

There are numerous reports of unusual psychological experiences in the Antarctic specially when one is alone, and I had a strange experience when I was returning to Little Scotland after my "house call". The blizzard was over and there was not even a puff of wind. The moon was full and the whole scene was really rather beautiful. It was totally silent, and I became aware of a strange sensation of fear which I could not understand but which I had been aware of on a few occasions before when alone and in silence. There was certainly no apparent reason for fear, and it was totally different from the previous night when there was every reason to be absolutely terrified rather than mildly afraid. I next became aware of an object a little way off on the ice shelf which greatly enhanced this feeling to something like panic. I knew there could be no living creature at that point, and I suppose feelings of the supernatural began to creep upon me. I think part of the problem was that I had no idea what the object was. It reminded me of the films made in the fifties about monsters which were quite terrifying until you saw them after which they lost their power. I could not identify this monster, however, so I took to my heels and fled. I discovered eventually that the object of my terror was nothing but a lump of brown paper! I am not sure whether the fear was caused by a kind of primeval fear of darkness or silence or even perhaps a combination of silence and darkness and whether it is akin to the partial withdrawal of sensory input in such circumstances. I have read of a very level-headed seaman on one of Scott's expeditions who developed such feelings of fear that he refused to be left alone under any circumstances.

We had been away from the main base for just over six weeks and during that time we carried letters from our colleagues at the main base to Little Scotland by sledge mail and had them authenticated by the postmaster of Halley Bay post office, George Lush. Some time before the Falkland Islands Dependencies post office service had been extended to incorporate the Antarctic bases. Halley Bay station was established by the Royal Society but when we took over it became a Falkland Islands Dependency Survey base, and George Lush was duly appointed postmaster. When he opened the post office for the first time we were able to have first day covers for all the letters we were preparing to send home when the ship came. The concept of sending a letter from Halley Bay by "sledge mail" was innovative, and I suppose it may be of some interest to a philatelist some day – particularly since Little Scotland or even Emperor Bay no longer exists.

Chapter 15

Midwinter

And so it was that after six very exciting weeks Mike and I packed up, stopped the generator, and made our way with our embryos back to the main base. When we entered we were immediately aware of a strange atmosphere. For one thing it was almost silent rather than being busy and bustling with people rushing along the corridors. I could not find anyone for a time, and eventually I discovered that they had all retracted into little hiding places either alone or in groups. There was no one in the lounge and even the close group which used to meet in my surgery was no longer there. Gordon was in his own little space under the eves and Jock was in his. Dennis was still bashing away at his radio, however, telling all who cared to listen what Hell it all was at −45 degrees within an ice shelf! The group which met in my surgery gradually re-formed but were very quiet and subdued. I found it quite difficult to get the other two out of a kind of depression into which they had gradually subsided. This was also common to the others. Even George spent most of his time alone in his office. In retrospect they all seemed to be suffering from a kind of depressive state. Life, however, had to go on, and I began to realize that Mike and I had been lucky to be away and very busy for the first half of the real winter. By this time I had a very nice new surgery constructed by George Lush in my absence, and I used to retire there after our evening meal. Shortly afterwards there would be a tap at the door and one of the chaps would come in. After a little bit of chat he would confess to being very depressed and unable to throw off a feeling of misery and uselessness. It took quite a bit of skill to talk him round but he would usually leave apparently feeling better. A short time after there was another tap and another would arrive with the same problem, and the performance was repeated many times. After I had seen more than half of the chaps and felt a bit drained myself I remember thinking, "Wait a minute, I am depressed too now and who is there to comfort me!"

The big celebration in the Antarctic is Midwinter Day. It takes precedence over Christmas Day and is an important landmark since there is always the possibility that we may just see a bit of sunlight again. We all made cards and little gifts for Midwinter, and Charlie really excelled when it came to the dinner. He made a cake which was a real work of art, and it depicted various aspects of the base in icing sugar. We not only had tinned fruit but a really terrific raspberry mouse. We were of course dressed up to the greatest extent possible – some even shaved a bit of their beard off, and George produced very fine wines that he had been storing for the occasion. We received messages from home and from the administration in London which had even sent a box of goodies only to be opened on Midwinter's Day. Most excitement was aroused when it was found that this box contained a can of Guinness for each base member. It was unfortunate that I did not like Guinness. In the afternoon we had a film show, and there was even a film we had not seen so we did not have to look at the *Three Musketeers* backwards.

During the celebrations which lasted for several days, a signal came from London to inform us that Apsley Cherry-Garrard had just died. I remember wondering who Cherry-Garrard was. I was not then aware that Mike and I had just completed the task he set out to achieve just over half a century before, and that I would consider his life and times on many occasions thereafter.

The Midwinter celebrations certainly did much to lift the depression from the base since there was so much preparation which involved everyone and we even all talked together again. After that people gradually sunk towards silence and depression again, but it was not nearly so bad as it had been. On 24 September at midday there was a sudden sound of raised, excited voices which split the silence of the hut. On investigation it transpired that a rim of sun had just peeped over the horizon. I cannot describe the joy we all felt at the sight of it. It banished the depression instantly and seemed to restore hope in the future. It is not difficult after an experience like that to see what led ancient people to worship the sun, and it possibly points to the origin of the depressions which commonly afflicts those who live in high latitudes.

Many years later when chronobiology became a science in its own right and implicated the pineal gland and its production of melatonin by light transmitted through the eyes, I thought of that day again. It is held that the seasonal affective disorder is caused by low light intensity acting on the pineal gland through the eyes and can be alleviated by increasing the intensity of light. We set up an experiment at Halley under the direction of Professor Josephine Arendt of the University of Surrey to test this in the field. I remember remarking that it was not necessary to implicate melatonin to account for winter depression in Antarctica, but the immediate powerful effect of the return of the sun certainly suggests that there is something very fundamental or biochemical about light on the human condition.

After the return of the sun, the base came to life again because there was still much to be done in addition to the repairs following the ravages of winter. From my point of view I had my physiological experiment to attend to and this in many ways was what I should have been concentrating on rather than chasing penguins. This had been on going since we arrived but following the completion of the penguin embryo programme I now devoted more energy and thought to this area. It entailed following four subjects around in rotation for twenty-four-hour periods. This was quite a marathon specially as most of my other work was physical, and I did not go to bed to prepare for the physiology but merely started in the evening after a full day of work digging out and re-siting stores etc. I had to carry on with the measurements for a full further twenty-four hours.

All this was particularly difficult in the middle of the night when everyone else had gone to bed. I had, however, found several big bottles of tablets in the surgery which were there to keep one going in case of an emergency or during the long days and nights of the relief. You see them in war films when people need to keep awake for a particular dangerous project. I started to take one of these capsules halfway through my long shift and they certainly kept me awake. What I also noticed was that they gave me a great feeling of well-being and confidence, and I felt myself breaking into very erudite discussions with whoever was willing to take part or listen. At the end of the thirty-six hours I was still mentally alert but felt physically shattered – though it did not seem to matter. The best part was going to bed and feeling a terrific sensation of peace as every part of my body relaxed, and I drifted off into a terrific sleep. You never hear about such drugs in these days of substance abuse. Fortunately, they did not appear to be addictive – but perhaps I did not take enough!

Chapter 16

The Physiological Manhaul Trip

At the back of my mind I had always harboured the ambition that my research work might one day lead to an MD, particularly as I was working for the MRC. Equally, my mother had told me that she considered one of the noblest occupations a man could have was medical research. I had little idea of the significance of my measurements at that time but I felt instinctively that I may not have enough material for a thesis, so I conceived the idea of setting up a manhaul sledge journey to conduct my measurements in the field under pretty tough physical conditions so that I could compare the maximum effort of polar life with the relatively sedentary position of life on a static base. First of all I consulted George Lush, and he was immediately supportive but suggested that I might do more than physiology and possibly do something in preparation for the proposed journey to the Dawson-Lampton glacier which was being planned for subsequent years. That seemed a good idea. I next spoke to Mick Blackwell who was also supportive of the scheme.

Thereafter I had to recruit the sledging party of four. The scientists readily agreed to cover each other's duties and that released Norman Hedderley and Gordon Artz. George Lush agreed to look after the generators and that released Jock. It was a good group. George now looked out a Nansen sledge, checked it out thoroughly, and loaded it up with provisions and primus stove etc. He also suggested that we had twice daily radio communications to test the radios in the field and carried a radar reflector on a long pole to determine whether it could be picked up by the Decca radar. Gordon did a survey of the ice shelf using a theodolite. Norman did the hourly meteorological observations in the same pattern as those carried out at the base, and he was also responsible for navigation and the planning of the route. In the featureless terrain of the ice shelf we had no special place to go. We could only be away for a week without putting too much strain on the resources of the base, so we just decided to go out and travel for two or three days, then change direction for a day, and finally return to the base during the final two or three days.

Mick also decided to allow me to carry out a survey of the vertical force of the earth's geomagnetic field using an instrument called a BMZ. This was a very delicate instrument which had not been transported in such a way before. (I was after all an assistant geomagnetic observer among my jobs!) The BMZ was mounted on the sledge in a specially prepared box surrounded by springs so that the effect of bumps and movement were minimised. There was a suspicion that there may be a mineral mass in the vicinity which was interfering with the routine magnetic observations. Mick hoped we could throw some light on this possibility. It is surprising what can turn up in the Antarctic and which can be difficult to explain. There was a very large, grounded iceberg close to the Halley area which was explored one winter and an empty Gordon's gin bottle was found on it. The berg was used as a reference point in some surveys and always referred to as the "gin bottle berg". The source of the gin bottle remained a mystery – as indeed did the brown paper which gave me a fright on the winter landscape.

On the physiological side I noted the activities of the group every fifteen minutes. Each man wore the temperature-sensitive vest in rotation each day. There had been a report that much weight was lost during sledge journeys although sufficient calories had apparently been provided. We, therefore, measured the calories we took in by noting carefully the composition of each meal and the amount of water each man drank. This was probably the most difficult part of the whole exercise, particularly since we had to weigh everything. I considered weighing each man each day, but in the end we settled for a pre-sledge weight and one taken immediately on return. It was thus a carefully worked-out field experiment, and we were quite proud of it, though this may not be the opinion of more experienced explorers!

Eventually we were ready to depart, and the whole base turned out to wish us well. It was a lovely day, and I really felt like the leader of an expedition as we set off. Navigation was done by dead reckoning using a milometer on a bicycle wheel and a compass on the sledge. We were soon out of sight of the base, and there were no landmarks to help as the ice shelf was completely featureless, and no horizon either since there was a continuous whiteout during the journey after the first day. Even the "gin bottle berg" disappeared from our sight during the first day. Fortunately there were no blizzards, and we only had to lie up for part on one day. I was pleasantly surprised on the evening of the sixth day when we actually found the base again, for our radio communications had not worked after the first day! The safe return was due to the navigation of Norman Hedderley. Since he was also the cook and we were well fed, he did a good job. I noticed that when he made porridge in the morning he added a liberal supply of sultanas and about half a pound of butter! This would have tasted pretty horrible at home, but presumably we needed the extra energy provided by the butter and the dried fruit to combat the cold and it tasted good. We were pretty comfortable in our sleeping bags at night and they remained dry. Classical explorers wrote about having to use up considerable energy to thaw out the ice which had collected in the bags from frozen sweat before they could get to sleep. This did not happen to us. Perhaps this was because our journey was relatively short – or possibly we were not working so hard! We did stop every hour to make a series of observations. Sleep had been difficult for some during the inactivity of the polar night but it was not a problem after a day of manhauling. One morning when I awoke from a deep sleep, I got into a panic because I could not move my head and thought I had become blind because I could only see featureless white. It transpired, however, that the fluid from my breath had frozen and fixed my head to the wall of the tent in such a way that my eyes were staring at the white tent wall.

The weather was reasonable for the trip, but we only had one really fine day when the sun shone brightly. For the rest of the time it blew slightly and there was no horizon. In other words only featureless white. I suppose it was a bit like the journeys to Emperor Bay but being light it was less disorientating – and of course much more comfortable since it was early summer. I must say that after we lost sight of the base I did wonder whether we would ever see it again especially since our navigation was entirely by dead reckoning.

Inspector John Duff who ran the Grampian Mountain Rescue team used to say that many of those who survived being lost in mountain blizzards were those who were so stupid as not to consider the danger they were in and the possibility that they may not survive. Since I seemed to have complete confidence in Norman's navigation and was not much concerned about danger I may well have been in that "Duff" classification! I was nevertheless quite pleased to see the base again after a week's absence.

When we got back, we had a great welcome from the others, and I realized that one of the biggest advantages of the trip for the base was that it gave everyone a new subject for discussion both while we were away and after we returned; it awakened the base members from the doom and gloom of winter and returned them to normal human beings. The break was also good for the sledge party for the same reason. I wondered afterwards whether that had been why George immediately reacted so positively to my suggestion of a trip. We had a party that night. The excuse was to celebrate our safe return – but not before we had all been weighed!

All of us lost several kilograms over the six days but it was largely replaced within twenty-four or forty-eight hours. That seemed to confirm that the weight loss was probably due to shortage of fluid. Part of the loss could have been due to the low humidity resulting in greater fluid losses from the lungs than usual. Another cause could have been the rapid evaporation of sweat since sweating certainly took place due to the heavy work of manhauling. It has also been suggested that since water has to be obtained by melting snow, part of the loss could be explained by saving fuel for this chore – but we were never thirsty.

These observations led to several interesting physiological studies in subsequent years where our findings were confirmed following long journeys. I wrote a report on our sledge journey at the end of the year. I suppose it was a bit over the top for we had only covered about 14 miles, and probably when Sir Vivian Fuchs read it he was quite justified in saying, "Stuff and bloody nonsense!" He had after all just journeyed across the whole continent and for the first time!

Chapter 17

The terminal phase

The days became longer as we approached the next summer and the end of the year. It was a time of great activity because the completion of the scientific programmes had to be achieved, the maintenance work following winter had to be done, the various food and equipment dumps had to be inspected and re-sited, the reports written and the indents for the next year made out and submitted. It was as well that this frenetic activity took place because it was rather a boring time since the big challenges had been faced up to and achieved, and there were few new things to look forward to. There had been no disasters and that was worth a good deal. Life on such a base is hard enough when things go well, but I often think of community problems when something goes really wrong or even when someone has lost his life. There was a particular occasion many years ago when a life was lost following a rather stupid prank at the beginning of the year and the group had to live together for the whole year before they were relieved. That must have been real hell and not only for the man responsible. My sympathy has always gone out to that group and to that man.

Charlie, the cook, joined in on all this hectic activity and preparations for the following year. He did finally achieve his big project of baking enough breakfast rolls for the whole of the next year. This meant that we had to enlarge the ice cave beside the kitchen to accommodate them. I never heard whether the new cook used them or baked his own. Charlie also wrote a report, and I remember being amused when

I saw it lying on a desk in the War Office when I returned to London marked "Top Secret" in red. In those days our food was all dehydrated or tinned and after a while proved not to be too appetizing. This was the place where he wrote in his report very proudly that he had been able to save ten cases of tinned fruit – the one real source of pleasure which we had! I am not sure whether he expected promotion, the Polar Medal, or the OBE for this saving, but it is just as well for his survival that his report was marked top secret.

Most people returning from the Antarctic are good cooks because we all had to be inventive to survive our day of cooking, and this has been reported to be the greatest source of stress in base life in Antarctica in many reports. We all had culinary secrets. Jock's pièce de résistance of mango chutney made from Lea and Perrins sauce and apricot jam went down very well when he produced it on his cook day. I had always had a partiality for apple rings fried in bacon fat, but when I tried it out on my day with dehydrated apple rings, it went down like a lead balloon. I did, however, use the tip from Rainer Goldsmith that a good squeeze of chlorophyll toothpaste imparted not only colour but an agreeable minty taste to dried peas.

When the daylight returned for long enough, several base members took to visiting Emperor Bay for a bit of exercise and fresh air or just to visit and photograph the remaining penguins. At first there was lots of activity as both parents rushed back and forwards from the sea with food for the chicks. It was difficult to see how far they had to walk to find open sea, but it was not long before we found that a hole had developed in the sea ice through which they could come and go. It is unlikely that this was made by the penguins themselves and much more likely that it was formed by a seal. During the winter there had been no sign of other life forms than emperor penguins, but in the spring and summer an occasional Weddell seal was to be found sunbathing on fine days. We got some idea of the underwater prowess of the penguins from observing them exiting the underwater locus through the blowhole. They must come up from depth at great speed, for they shoot out of the water for several feet and land on the edge of the blow hole on their feet before waddling off. They have been said to fly through the water like underwater birds using their flippers as wings but the flippers must almost act as propellers to allow such speed to be generated. They are awkward on the ice surface, but if pursued, they flop onto their bellies and are then able to move much faster using their wings like canoe paddles.

Presumably one of the reasons for choosing such a very southerly place for their reproductive activity is the absence of predators of any kind. This, however, has a cost because there was a fairly high maternal mortality rate noted when the sun came back. The surface of the bay was very messy and a bit smelly with the excrement of many months and the bodies of adult dead penguins and a much greater number of dead chicks. It was not clear whether the maternal mortality was due to environmental or obstetric factors – or even if the corpses were all females because it is only possible to sex a penguin by carrying out an autopsy – at least for us! Some of the adult corpses may, of course, have been males dying of exposure and starvation since the sea ice was late to break up. The reason for raising an obstetric possibility was the presence of blood around the cloaca of some of the corpses.

Another cause of infant mortality soon became apparent, however. This was the powerful parenting instincts of the adults. When it became clear that there was a shortage of chicks, there was an almighty scramble for any chick walking about on its own. Emperor penguins are not normally aggressive, but this all changes at this time of the year and the scramble is so great that it frequently ends in the demise of the chick. Unlike other animals the chicks are probably reared in a kind of nursery. When a bird returns with food, it is not clear whether it really recognizes its own chick as we thought or just selects any chick which it feeds and adopts for a while proudly displaying it on its feet like an egg. This seems the more likely explanation since it was an embryo in an egg when it left on the third post-partum day. This is fine until there is a scarcity of chicks and then the fun begins. The fewer the chicks the greater the slaughter of the survivors from ill-advised attempts at adoption. Wilson noted the high mortality rate of chicks at Cape Crozier in 1902 and estimated that at least 70 per cent of the chicks died. The same proportion or even more probably died at Emperor Bay in 1959 for there were very few left at midsummer.

In late summer the sea ice in Emperor Bay broke up and

disappeared leaving no evidence of the breeding activity and the frenetic scrambles of the summer. By the time the new ice formed, there would be no indication for new arrivals that this had been a scene of enormous activity when the sun set and the blizzards of winter arrived. This is probably why it was not until the twentieth century that the first breeding site of these magnificent creatures was discovered at Cape Crozier. On our way home our ship did pass several emperor penguins hitching a lift on ice floes or on small icebergs.

We had heard that the Royal Research Ship (RRS) *John Biscoe* was coming to collect us, and we all hoped and prayed that she would make it. She was a flat-bottomed ship which had been built in Paisley and launched broadside into the river Cart. The superstructure was high presumably to see over the ice and this made her a poor sea boat. On one trip the only man who was not sick in Southampton water was the captain, and I have seen a man catapulted from the depth of an overstuffed armchair in the wardroom and bounced off the bulkhead opposite – albeit in a pretty rough sea. If *John Biscoe* made it, she would be the first British ship to get so far south since Shackleton's *Endurance* was beset and lost at about the same latitude in the Weddell Sea.

In time we became aware that *John Biscoe* had entered the ice and was making good progress. This provided a new subject for us and from that time discussions largely centred around where she was and whether she had got stuck and where. One morning without warning, however, when we were having breakfast Dennis Savins burst in shouting that the *Biscoe* had just sighted Halley Bay. This was unexpected, and we all rushed out and jumped on a tractor sledge and proceeded with all speed to the sea ice. There she was and when we arrived, the crew were anchoring her to a berth in the ice. Suddenly instead of rushing to talk to different people, we hung back in a heap and felt strangely shy. It was unexpected but we did not really want to talk to these new people and could think of little to say to them. Fortunately that problem soon passed.

John Biscoe was a different style of ship from *Tottan*. For one thing the officers were all in uniform, and there was the feeling of "rigid, destroyer discipline", as Captain Scott described how he ran his expedition. The first officer was Tom Woodward, and he presided over the wardroom while Captain Johnson remained in his own quarters above. The base personnel (known as Fids) were housed in the "Fiddery", and the seamen had their own quarters also. There was thus a kind of pecking order or class structure which was quite appealing particularly if one found oneself in the upper class. I was to be the medical officer of the ship, so I had a cabin of my own next to the surgery, and I was to be a member of the wardroom and eat there. The others were accommodated in two- or four-berth cabins and ate in the Fiddery. It had been suggested to me before I left that if we sailed south on the *Biscoe*, it could cause problems later if one was an officer on the ship and then had to join the egalitarian bunch on the base on arrival. I was, however, going home and I loved the concept – though I did not say so to my colleagues. It was certainly an improvement on the five man each side in the forecastle on *Tottan*.

After the initial introductions and discussions we had lunch on *John Biscoe*, but thereafter it was to be the same rush as before on the *Tottan* to get the cargo offloaded and our boxes on board so that the ship could get out before the shore lead froze over. Lunch was fantastic. It transpired that the cook was a chef at the Savoy who had signed on for a trip to see the Antarctic. I was thus quite glad to evacuate Halley and take up residence on the ship and the wardroom. My relief doctor – one Charles Forrest MD – was a good bit older than the rest of us and had served for about ten years in the colonial medical service. He was sophisticated and the thought of the manual labour of unloading did not appeal too much. When he settled down on a massive armchair in the wardroom after lunch and placed a red handkerchief with white spots over his face for a nap as was his wont after lunch, the first officer was not amused and ordered him into the hold to commence unloading. He was thus very willing to take up residence on the base and to take care of the base while I assumed responsibility for the ship. It was rumoured that when he reported at Southampton he had the third officer carry his bag to his quarters!

We were spared the blizzard that broke up the sea ice the previous year, but the sea ice did indeed break up a few days after the ship's arrival. On this occasion, however, there were no personnel, tractors, or stores on the ice and it was all much less exciting. I was given one of the tractors to drive up and down – you will recall I was assistant diesel mechanic, and by this time, an experienced driver and polar traveller, no less! We worked round the clock as before, and the weather was a bit questionable at times. One day when it was becoming more and more difficult to see through the drifting snow, I was proceeding towards the boat with a full load when I became aware that I was not recognising the usual landmarks and indeed could see very little in front of me. A sixth sense made me stop and get off to investigate. I was horrified to find that I was right at the edge of the ice shelf. Another few yards forward and I would have plunged 200 feet down to the sea ice. Once again my guardian angel had clicked in, and it emphasised just how dangerous the Antarctic can be.

The unloading proceeded without further incident when the weather moderated and in record time it was complete. The handover to our opposite numbers took place, and we were ready to depart. I had already personally transported my precious box of penguin embryos to the surgery on the ship and stowed it in a safe place. I refused to allow it to be put into the hold, but I could not prevent the larger box of physiological equipment and data sheets from being placed in the hold. That box, however, was moved from ship to ship on the way home, and it eventually reached London after being reported lost for more than three months during its journey. If that had happened to my penguin embryos, I think I would have needed psychiatric treatment.

The day came for us to sail but we did not steam out and away. Instead we went a little further south because Captain Johnson said he wanted to see Emperor Bay. He told me that he wished to take some emperor penguins back to Vancouver Zoo and had a biologist with him to help look after them on the journey. When we got to Emperor Bay, there were only one or two rather moth-eaten penguins still in residence, and the captain told me to jump over the side and catch them. I jumped and twisted my knee when I landed so that I could not run after the beasts. They had taken off at a swift belly flop for the further reaches of the bay in any case. As the boat was not stopping I climbed back aboard by catching a dangling rope in the nick of time.

Captain Johnson was an Irishman and as much of a character as Captain Jacobsen of the *Tottan* and just as good a sailor, for *Biscoe* was no better suited for the Deep South than the *Tottan*. We did not have the same series of riotous parties as we had with the Norwegians when we arrived, and I suppose we were both glad and sorry to leave the ice shelf which had been our home for the past one year. When we majestically sailed past the party we were leaving behind on the sea ice, they looked very vulnerable. That moment of schadenfreude was very emotional, and when the ship rendered its usual three sonorous blasts on the whistle, there were few dry eyes on the ship.

We were now on our way home and had time to reflect on our experiences. In many ways they became more important to me with the passage of time. The difficult, boring, and uncomfortable bits were soon forgotten and the central theme of achievement and comradeship predominated. When I thought of my two research projects, the penguin embryos and the physiology, I was acutely aware that they were nearly disasters but both were saved by the selfless help I had had from my colleagues. I have since thought that an Antarctic research project is particularly rewarding because it is very difficult and often only achieved after terrific persistence and the co-operation of like-minded individuals. The experience I had has remained a central experience of my life, and what it means to me is best summed up in the last paragraph of Cherry-Garrard's great book, *The Worst Journey in the World:*

"And I tell you, if you have the desire for knowledge and the power to give it physical expression, go out and explore. Some will tell you that you are mad, and nearly all will say: "What is the use?" For we are a nation of shopkeepers, and no shopkeeper will look at research that does not promise him a financial return within a year. And so you will sledge nearly alone, but those with whom you sledge will not be shopkeepers: that is worth a good deal. If you march your winter journeys, you will have your reward, so long as all you want is a penguin's egg."

Fifty years later I cannot read that paragraph with a dry eye. The modern view of research is even more governed by the economic, shopkeeper philosophy than ever in the past. University academic medicine has thus lost a good deal of the substance which produced the great British medical tradition.

Caboose mounted on a Maudheim sledge and about to be towed to Emperor Bay. The temperature was –43 deg. C.

Bamboo canes with flags mark the route between Halley Bay and Emperor Bay. Note the rime encrusted telephone wire which joins them to each other and which is used to help find the next bamboo during blizzards and winter darkness.

Little Scotland in winter. It was sited on the cliff overlooking the rookery in Emperor Bay. The generator is on the left.

Flash photograph taken at mid-day of penguins in the typical winter huddle. Some are obviously incubating eggs. Photographer, HJ Jones, 1971. Reproduced courtesy of BAS-NERC. British Antarctic Survey Archives Service. Ref. AD6/19/3/Wp21.

Penguin in dexion cage on sea ice patiently incubating an embryo.

Placing an egg in a sea-boot stocking for safe transport to the caboose on the cliff above.

Dissecting the embryo from the egg in the caboose.

RRS John Biscoe at sea near Deception Island en route to bring us home. Photographer, HAD Cameron, 1959. Reproduced courtesy of NERC-BAS. British Antarctic Survey Archives Service. Ref. AD6/19/3/B25.

Returning penguins taking a short cut courtesy of a hole in the sea ice probably created by a seal.

RRS John Biscoe anchored to sea ice at Halley Bay, 1959, and preparing for homeward voyage. The first British ship to penetrate so far South since Shackleton's Endurance was lost in the same area of the Weddell Sea.

Chapter 18

The Royal Research Ship *John Biscoe*

Life on *John Biscoe* was different from *Tottan*. Since I was recognised as the ship's medical officer and as one of the officers I could not avoid a feeling of mild superiority. The wardroom was very British with the first officer at the head of the table, and the officers were always in uniform. The food was terrific. Everyone fought over the fantastic buttered asparagus tips, and there were such delicacies as roast pheasant. It was so genuine that it often still had the lead shot in it. This was great until we got out of the ice, for the *Biscoe* was not good in rough weather, and that is putting it very mildly.

We were heading for South Georgia. The captain appointed me Penguin Officer and was intent on taking a dozen emperor penguins back to Vancouver Zoo. My first job was to catch them. A day or two later I was lying on my bunk nursing the sore knee I had twisted when I jumped on to the sea ice at Emperor Bay and thinking that we were running out of sea ice and thus available penguins. I was imperiously summoned to the bridge. The captain pointed out a relatively small ice flow on which stood a solitary emperor penguin. He said, "I want it. I cannot stop so you will have to jump on to the flow when I get the ship as close as I can." When I got to the deck, I noticed that in addition to the penguin on the flow, there was a black head in the water close by watching it. I wondered whether it was a killer whale or a leopard seal looking for its dinner but felt that I could do little else but have a go particularly when the captain leaned over the wing of the bridge and yelled, "Jump." So I jumped.

As I landed on this little flow the penguin, of course, jumped off. I now had two twisted knees, and I could see the ship slipping past the flow. I had heard of people being put on a sand bank on the Mississippi but to be left on a tiny ice flow in the Weddell Sea seemed a bit beyond a joke. Just as the ship was disappearing I noticed a rope hanging down from the deck, so I grabbed it. I was never very good at rope climbing but I certainly shinned up that rope very rapidly – even with two twisted knees!

Eventually we came across two icebergs joined together by a sheet of sea ice upon which there were several groups of emperors. I, of course, knew all about chasing and incarcerating emperor penguins and as the Penguin Officer I supervised the hunt, the placement of the hostages in large bags, and their transport back to the ship. Happily, we now had our two dozen penguins, and there was no longer any need for me to leap off the ship to tiny ice flows. We had already built an enclosure on the deck to house any penguins we could catch. It had a wooden frame, and the enclosure was completed with the ubiquitous chicken netting. The Canadian biologist now appeared – although I do not recall him at the catching part. He now took charge explaining that the usual diet of emperor penguins was krill but we did not have any, so it was necessary to change the diet to whale meat of which we had an abundant supply. The penguins were not impressed, so the biologist and I had to feed them. This involved one of us – usually me – getting a penguin between my legs and opening its mouth while the other insinuated a long slither of whale meat down its gullet. This was a terrible struggle at first, and I was black and blue, for the birds could weigh a hundredweight and there were two dozen to feed each day. Mercifully, however, they got used to it and feeding became easier until eventually they opened their mouths without persuasion and took their dinner without demur.

Grytviken in South Georgia was our first port of call. When we arrived there we were told that we had to go home via Cape Town. That seemed a great idea but a day later we were informed that we had to go to Port Stanley first because we had been invited to a cocktail party at Government House. That meant a week of sailing through the roaring forties in the flat-bottomed *John Biscoe* and a week sailing back to South Georgia! It was said that this was not just a courtesy visit to the governor but because we had to change ship to the RRS *Shackleton* which was at Port Stanley. I thought it would have been a better idea to wait at South Georgia till the Shackleton arrived, but that idea was not entertained. In retrospect I think it may have been something to do with the arrangements which the captain had made for the onward transportation of his penguins to Vancouver. This included a transfer to the MS *Darwin*, which plied between Port Stanley and Montevideo and then a rush across that city to a refrigerated compartment on a plane bound for Vancouver. The arrangements had been made with meticulous care.

I had a great respect for Captain Johnson who was not only a great seaman but a fantastic raconteur. He used to come down to the wardroom occasionally in the evenings to chat to Dr Gordon DeQ Robin the director of the Scott Polar Institute in Cambridge, who was visiting the Antarctic at that time, and I would listen spellbound to their stories. In any event, when the *Biscoe* returned to Southampton later that year I rushed down to meet her because I was keen to hear what had become of the penguins. The captain gave me a drink, shook his head sadly, and said, "They all died, Doc." I was sorry to hear that after all our hard work, but I thought little more about it. A couple of years later, however, someone who visited Vancouver and knew of my interest in penguins remarked that he had seen the first collection of emperor penguins in captivity in Vancouver Zoo. It was rumoured that the captain had sold them for £200 a head!

Captain Johnson ran his ship like a Royal Navy destroyer but he was a merchant seaman and had very little time for the Royal Navy. There was always a Royal Navy ship in British Antarctic waters and at that time it was HMS *Protector*. We never seemed to have anything to do with these ships, however, and the personnel were never invited aboard the Survey vessels. The captain reckoned that he was not in need of protecting. The Royal Navy sailors were always keen to have a look at the expedition ship but were frightened of the wrath of our captain if they neared it. One afternoon when we were moored alongside the *Protector* in Port Stanley, Captain Johnson went ashore in civilian clothes to visit someone, and he left his cap on the wardroom table. A few of us were having a drink to pass the time, and looking out of the window we saw half a dozen matelots cautiously climbing over the forward part of *Protector* to the *Biscoe*, which was moored alongside. One of the lads picked up the captain's cap, ran up to the bridge, peered over the wing showing a mass of gold-scrambled egg, and in a gruff voice bellowed, "Get off my fucking boat." In the panic-stricken retreat, one of them nearly ended up in the water.

Our stay at South Georgia was short. It allowed a quick return visit to Shackleton's monument and his grave among the whalers, and it marked the end of the calm seas. The journey to Port Stanley was as expected but the seas could have been even rougher. The excellent food was no longer looked forward to as it was in the calmness of the ice. Being a British ship one could not indicate any weakness by admitting to the possibility of seasickness, so I forced myself from my bunk at dinner times, struggled along to the ward room, ate as little as possible, and retired via the heads to be sick on the way back to my bunk. Mercifully, the penguins were able to take their whale meat dinners without my presence by that time.

Arriving at Port Stanley we duly had our terminal cocktail party with Sir Arrow Smith in Government House, and I was surprised and pleased that he remembered all our names and asked sensible and interested questions about our year. It was a much quieter affair than our previous visit, and we quickly transferred to the Shackleton with Captain Turnbull and once again set sail for South Georgia. The Shackleton had fine lines and was no better in rough weather than the *Biscoe* – and the cook was not a Savoy chef. Once again I had a cabin to myself as part of the medical suite which was very nice. I was disappointed, however, to find that I was no longer a member of the wardroom – indeed I do not know whether this ship had a wardroom. It was run on much more egalitarian principles than the *Biscoe*. An oceanographic survey was being carried out for the admiralty by a retired Royal Navy commander who was obviously enjoying the trip, especially as the measurements were to be made by us – and not him – every fifteen minutes on four-hour watches and – insult of insults – the medical officer was expected to take his turn!

When we arrived at South Georgia this time, it was to the other whaling station called Leith, which seemed much bigger and busier than Grytviken. There seemed to be massive steam plants and engines with machinery everywhere. It all looked very dangerous and miserable to live in. I could see the point of banning alcohol as I looked at the activity. Whaling certainly must have made lots of money, for the new massive organ in St Giles Cathedral in Edinburgh was installed by the Salvesen family which had owned a South Georgia whaling station.

After a short time, we left South Georgia for the third time and proceeded north-east at last for Cape Town, which we reached a couple of weeks later after a short stop at Tristan Da Cunha. I was on duty one night surveying the ocean floor, and the instrument had been jogging along, quietly showing a depth of several thousand feet, when it suddenly went mad with depths swinging all over the place. The readings rapidly decreased until coming close to the surface, it transpired that we had arrived at Tristan Da Cunha. Here we had to pick up the district administrator, Mr Day, and transport him and his family to Cape Town. Tristan Da Cunha consisted of a great rock with a little shelf on one side and no harbour or jetty. The Day family with their belongings were duly rowed out by the locals and boarded the ship. The Tristans looked a bit like the planet of the apes and though they were said to be descended from the crew of a wrecked Scottish ship they had become coloured over the years. They were therefore not welcomed in neighbouring South Africa at that time. They were very good fishermen, however, and had access to crayfish which the South Africans were very glad to welcome and loved to buy. So the Tristans had become wealthy. There was nothing to spend their money on, however. They had fridges and cookers but no source of power for them! The community was not unlike St Kilda but their resources and space were more limited. Nevertheless when they were evacuated some years later they fared no better than the St Kildans, and many of the older people actually returned.

The weather got progressively better and a small group of us were talking about buying an old car and driving up Africa on the way home but that plan had to be aborted when Jock's fiancée Edith sent a signal to say that she was coming out to Cape Town to meet him and suggested that they should get married in Cape Town. Without Jock it would have been madness to attempt to drive through Africa at that time. We were compensated somewhat, however, by a signal which came from London to say that we would return on a Union Castle boat but would need to stay in Cape Town for two weeks and asked if we had any preference for hotels. Presumably they had forgotten that we had two South Africans in our party, so we asked Gordon which was the best hotel in Cape Town, and he gave us the name of a very fine establishment at Seapoint, and much to our surprise we were booked into it. Things were certainly looking up, especially as the weather remained good. We first saw Table Mountain as the sun was setting. It was a beautiful sight and when the tug came out to meet us, there was Edith on the bow, and she jumped aboard as soon as possible. Jock introduced her to me with the words, "Well, here she is, Doc – no' much to look at but she has an awful kind heart."

We had a great time in Cape Town. I do not think I have seen a more beautiful city or surroundings. The hotel was terrific. The normal restaurant served ten-course dinners, and there was also a very special restaurant which served fabulous food. There was a wonderful swimming pool just along the road where I was amazed to see tiny kids swimming at the deep end and climbing up to the top diving board and diving in. It was very different from the icy cold Storie Street baths that I had been used to in Paisley. (That was probably one of the reasons why none of my family could swim well.) In line with the beautiful surroundings of Cape Town I thought the girls were just about the best looking that I had ever seen. Perhaps it was the tan they were all able to acquire, the lovely clothes they wore, or just that I had not seen a member of the opposite sex for over a year, but I do not think so.

When Jock's wedding came along, I was invited to be the best man. Not having much experience at that sort of thing I asked the manager how much champagne we should have since there were only eight guests, and the reception was to be at noon since the appointment at the registrar's office was for a little before that time. The manager suggested that to be on the safe side we should put eight bottles in the fridge, and he would take back what we did not use. I agreed. There were the usual problems – the decree for his divorce was not there but after much phoning we got the problem sorted, and they were duly married. When we returned, we had all this to talk about and the eventual success of the marriage to celebrate. I was then tapped on the shoulder by the head waiter who said there is no more champagne left! It was then that it dawned on us that we were all plastered! The celebration was thus put on hold while we all went off for a swim and a sleep, and we agreed to meet on the main veranda or stoep for a drink before dinner which had been arranged in the very fancy restaurant.

We met at the appointed hour, and it transpired that there had been an article in the paper about the girl who had come out from England to marry her fiancée from the Antarctic, complete with her picture. One man came up and offered his congratulations. Jock was delighted and immediately invited him for dinner with his partner. I then had to go in and ask the head waiter to set another two places at the table and go for more money. Then another came over and the performance was repeated, and this was followed by a third who was also invited for dinner. I was just wondering how to cope with this when Jock stood on his chair and announced to the considerable crowd present that this was his wedding day and they were all invited for dinner. I gave up after that and just enjoyed my dinner.

Before we left Cape Town I visited the Africaans University at Stellenbosch, and I have never seen such a magnificent university campus – especially when compared with what we were used to at the University of Glasgow. They had swards of green lawn, swimming pools, tennis courts, and bright airy and spacious labs. I had gone there to present the department of zoology with a penguin embryo, and Professor Du Toit invited me to address the students – much to my consternation. We also had a visit to Gordon's brother's house and had a braaivleis, or barbecue, in his beautiful garden. I had never experienced this form of eating and entertaining at that time, and I thought it was marvellous. I have tried to emulate it when I am in a hot country, but I have never achieved Geoffrey Artz' performance or anything like it.

We returned to Britain on the Union Castle ship Caernarvon Castle. I chanced my arm by suggesting that I should go first class since I was an Army officer, but that cut no ice. On the ship three-quarters of the accommodation was first class, and there were nine first class passengers, eight of whom appeared to be in their nineties. The ninth was a young lad who used to jump the barrier to the tourist section at the back where the action was. The voyage took a couple of weeks. There was no room to sit out on deck when we went through the warm weather, and when it got cold north of the Canary Islands there was loads of room on deck but none inside. We did, however, stop at Las Palmas on this occasion and that made up for missing it on the way out. Rough weather did not bother the Caernarvon Castle, but it seemed to bother a large number of passengers. Perhaps, I thought, I am not such a bad sailor after all. When we got back to Southampton, there was Margaret and Jim- – now Mr and Mrs Gassor – to meet me very close to the spot where they had seen me off a year and a half before on *Tottan*. It had been a great adventure, but it was also great to be home.

Chapter 19

Delivery of the penguin embryos to London

I had thirteen boxes including two boxes of penguin egg shells and my very precious box of penguin embryos. Somehow we got them to Cheltenham in Jim's diminutive motor car. I was not charged duty by the customs on my egg shells but on practically everything else, so I was not in the best of moods when I emerged from the customs shed. It was very nice to spend the first night back in a normal British house, but next morning I took the train to London with my box of embryos and arrived at the department of anatomy at Charing Cross Hospital. The taxi crossing London did not crash – as had been my recurring nightmare in Antarctica – neither was the enthusiastic Dr Glenister standing on the front steps to meet me. I was informed politely but rather coldly by a secretary that he was now in fact the Professor of Anatomy and a very busy man. I was, therefore, invited to leave the embryos and my report with a technician and basically just to go away. I did this rather reluctantly and unhappily, and I never heard anything more from Professor Glenister though I did think that he could at least have written a short note of thanks considering what we had gone through to produce the embryos. I enquired several times over the years and was persistently told by FIDS that the embryos were being worked upon.

It was at least a little better than the response which Cherry-

Garrard got when he took his three precious embryos to the Natural History Museum half a century before. In the *Worst Journey in the World* he described how Dr Wilson and a professor at the Natural History Museum had been fascinated by the concept that the emperor penguin may be the evolutionary link between birds and reptiles, and they developed an almost obsessive, burning interest to obtain some embryos to investigate this. Until the beginning of the twentieth century emperor penguins had been seen and described standing on ice floes on the Southern Ocean not infrequently. There was no knowledge of their nesting or breeding habits. In 1902, however, during Captain Scott's Discovery expedition, Edward Wilson discovered the first breeding rookery to be described when he accidentally happened upon it in the obscure bay at Cape Crozier. There were a few chicks still present, and he concluded from their development that the eggs must have been laid in June or July which is of course the depth of winter.

Emperor penguins do not nest but lay their eggs on the sea ice and then nurse them on their feet. It has been said that these creatures never walk on land. That may or may not be true but the entire breeding process is completed on sea ice and at the end of winter when the sea ice in the bay breaks up it takes all evidence of the breeding activity with it. This is presumably why it took so long to discover how they bred. Several other rookeries have been found subsequently. The one adjacent to Halley Bay was particularly large, but whole bays disappear from time to time as icebergs. So new rookeries have to be sought when that happens.

During Scott's last expedition Wilson recruited his assistant zoologist, Apsley Cherry-Garrard and Lieutenant Bowers to help him obtain some specimens. They set out during winter on a 70-mile journey to Cape Crozier. *The Worst Journey in the world* describes the incredible privations and terrible sufferings the small party endured. They eventually arrived at a cliff overlooking the rookery on the sea ice. In atrocious weather they only had time to abseil down to the sea ice and at the third attempt they managed to grab five eggs. But two of them were smashed on the return journey. They had built a small hut of rocks as shelter because they intended to spend some time there collecting eggs. That night, however, a great blizzard arrived and their tent was blown away. Knowing they would not survive the return journey without a tent they set about looking for the remnants of the tent when the blizzard abated some days later and by great good fortune they found it. They had lost all their other kit, however, so they concentrated on survival and just made it back to Cape Evans having narrowly escaped with their lives. In fact Cherry-Garrard was the only one of the three to return from the main expedition alive. It was very different from our expedition.

When Cherry-Garrard arrived at the Natural History Museum in 1913 with his offering, he was in fact received rudely and told that Wilson's professor was now dead and that no one else was interested in the project. This was a terrible blow and only when Captain Scott's formidable sister accompanied him and banged the table at the museum were the embryos accepted and a Professor Assheton assigned to work them up. Cherry-Garrard went off to war in the trenches of France. Meanwhile, Professor Assheton died before he could address the task. Thereafter the embryos seemed to have disappeared into obscurity.

Nearly fifteen years later when I was in a position to consider the matter further and was a research director myself I went to the British Antarctic Survey (as FIDS was known by that time), expressed my concern, and asked for my embryos back saying that I would find an interested embryologist and we would work them up between us. This was agreed but when it asked for the embryos, the Survey was told that a technician had accidentally disposed of them! This was shattering news and put me in much the same position as Cherry-Garrard. He had gone off to war, and I had gone off to train as a surgeon. Sadly, in both cases the embryos appeared to have been lost. It now looked as though history had been repeated and my endeavours had come to the same end point. Cherry-Garrard had, however, written his great book describing an amazing feat of human endeavour which is still consulted with wonder to this day. My experience had taught me a great deal about the trials and troubles of research, the need for persistence to overcome obstacles, and the thrill of eventual achievement. This stood me in good stead for the rest of my professional, academic life. I suspect that both of us gained a great deal from our experiences.

A century after the publication of *The Worst Journey in the World*

I could not help wondering what was so special about the emperor penguin and its embryology that such a man as the gentle scientist Edward Wilson was so obsessed with it that he was able to persuade such characters as Birdie Bowers and Apsley Cherry-Garrard to accompany him on this desperate, life-threatening expedition. The opportunity to add to existing knowledge was strong motivation for members of Scott's expedition which was, unlike Amundsen's party, strongly involved in scientific discovery. The discovery of the rookery and the elucidation of the penguin's breeding habits were of considerable interest but the embryological aspect provided much additional importance and a vital reason for the famous winter journey. The Scott expeditions were in the same time scale as Charles Darwin's voyage of the Beagle and his theory of natural selection was still being violently debated by both scientists and the church. Wilson had brought some specimens of emperor penguins home on Discovery since he was convinced that they may just be the oldest birds in existence and therefore of much importance in evolution. His excitement was further raised when it appeared that they had some embryonic features of reptiles, fish, and birds, and it was not clear whether they were amphibious fish, flying reptiles or aquatic birds. He therefore determined to get some real embryos and started making plans to obtain them well before setting sail on Terra Nova on Captain Scott's last expedition.

Subsequent study of emperor penguins has revealed that they are indeed amazing creatures. They walk up to 120 kilometres over sea ice to their breeding grounds every winter. The female loses 25 per cent of her body weight even before she lays an egg. The male incubates the egg for an average of 115 days and loses about 40 per cent weight. Also, they can dive as deep as 265 metres (896 feet) in search of food – that is as deep as the average saturation diver in the North Sea achieves – but he takes more than a week to return to the surface! The emperor penguin achieves its dive in one breath and that is presumably why it does not develop decompression sickness. Wilson noted that the mortality of chicks seemed very high and placed it at about 77 per cent of live births. Stonehouse, working at Marguerite Bay on the Antarctic Peninsula agreed but cast doubt on the magnitude of the mortality figure placing it a nearer 30 per cent. Marguerite Bay is of course much further north and the mortality noted at Emperor Bay by us was closer to Wilson's figure while the Scottish National Museum in Edinburgh places it in the region of 90 per cent.

We can thus now understand something of the obsession which drove Wilson. He had discovered the breeding grounds of the emperor penguin and as a zoologist living in the controversial scientific times which accompanied Darwin's violently debated theories of evolution, he stood to uncover a scientific discovery of great contemporary importance. This would certainly have added much value to the scientific outcome of Scott's expedition. It is unfortunate that Professor Assheton died before he could approach the task of examining the eggs. Presumably Professor Glenister had the idea of completing the project.

My penguin project was conducted in difficult circumstances but in much greater comfort and safety due to the time taken for preparation and the support of many colleagues. The results were better in that the whole series of embryos requested was obtained but little of scientific value came of them. Presumably the facts of evolution were now less controversial. It provided me with a fantastic apprenticeship in research technique, however, which served me well all my professional life. It is not always the actual result of research which provides satisfaction but the intellectual energy and passion spent in achieving the result. That is why research is such an important component of training for any aspect of professional life. Those responsible for directing and funding research today do not always appreciate or accept this. Cherry-Garrard was presumably as disappointed as I was that our penguin projects did not reveal more. But as he said, "You will have your reward, as long as all you want is a penguin's egg."

Chapter 20

Isolation in Hampstead

After a weekend in Cheltenham I proceeded to the HQ officers' mess at Millbank and was told to go off for six weeks disembarkation leave and then to return to work up my research results at the MRC labs. Being a romantic at heart I spent the night at the beautiful mess and imagined I was Phileas Fogg returning to the Reform Club after his journey around the world. I also sought out Per August's restaurant in Soho and had the same meal as I had the night before I sailed – once again in the guise of Phileas Fogg! The next day I returned to Cheltenham to pick up my twelve remaining boxes and took a sleeper north. I had to change at Crewe and had to get my boxes into the train in the middle of the night. In those days the second class sleeper had four berths – it was worse than the forecastle of the *Tottan*. Mercifully only one of the other berths was occupied! The next morning when I got to Inverness my mother was on the platform to meet me. I got a bit of a shock because for the first time ever I realised that she was no longer young. It was a bit of an emotional reunion. My father told me later that she had become silent and withdrawn halfway through my absence, and it had transpired that for some administrative reason my pay had not been paid into the bank for a couple of months, and she assumed that this was because I was dead and no one had bothered to tell them. She had kept it very much to herself because she had not wished to upset my father.

My six weeks in Tain were wonderful. I took my favourite walk up to Tarlogie and back several times. This was the walk which I used to take when I came to Tain as a student and needed sorting out after being thwarted in love or having some sort of professional disaster which needed consideration and thought. In those days that walk always worked for me in the times of the intense mental suffering which young people have to endure as they grow up. Towards the end of the six weeks, I was informed that the case which contained the results of my physiology had been transferred to a ship at Montevideo. It had now docked at Southampton. But my box had disappeared, so there was little point in returning to work up the results.

I was very annoyed and asked where the ship was now and whether I could go and search for it myself. I was told that it was an old ship which had now gone to be broken up and that there was little point. In a way I was not too upset because I had no idea what I was going to do with the data anyway, and I could now do something about getting on with my surgical training. I went to my old hospital in Glasgow – the Victoria Infirmary – and saw the medical superintendent Dr Cameron Wemyss and explained the problem. He offered me a job as senior house officer in orthopaedics – the branch of surgery about which I knew least! As I was about to leave Tain to take up this appointment, however, I got a further note from the Army in London to say that my box had now turned up and that I should proceed to London forthwith to do something with it. I was tempted to tell them to throw it in the river but I rather reluctantly agreed to return. It transpired that although the old boat had taken six weeks to transfer my box from Montevideo to Southampton, British Road Transport had taken a full eight weeks to transfer it from Southampton to London. Apparently there were four depots between Southampton and London, and my box had lain for some time at each of them and thus had taken longer to travel from Southampton to London than it took to travel from the Antarctic to Southampton!

I had to admit that it was rather nice to be back in the mess and in London. In those days one became a captain in the second year of National Service – no one told me about promotion so I just sewed an additional pip on my uniform and became a captain – at least everyone called me captain and I was paid as a captain. When I got to the labs at Hampstead, however, there was no one there except the cleaner and a previous FID who was just leaving. I took his desk and unpacked my box. The cleaner told me that everyone had gone to Aden to carry out some trials on heat for the Army and they would be away for about six weeks. It appeared that with the shrinkage of the empire, the government was aware that we no longer had a toehold in a hot country. If the nation was required to take military action to sort out a problem in a hot country, we now had no troops acclimatised to heat. The MRC had been contracted by the War Office to undertake some research into artificial acclimatisation to heat, and the whole division had taken off for Aden with a regiment of soldiers to see if their laboratory experiments worked in the field.

That was a blow because I did not know where to start. My first weeks in London were very lonely and miserable because there was no one to talk to, and I had a limited amount in common with the cleaner. I had nothing to do at work, and when I got back to the mess I found that the next man up was a full colonel, and none of these very senior officers were much interested in talking to me either. I walked about the streets but no one talked to me there. I started to go to pubs but though one could occasionally exchange a few words there it did not lead to anything. I therefore went to the pictures and that passed the time. For a time I spent the morning with the paper deciding where I would go that evening and then as the boredom increased I started going to the pictures in the afternoon and again in the evening. I had to work further and further out from the centre until eventually there was nothing else to see. The effect of all this was that during the next decade in Scotland there were few films that I had not already seen!

It must have been about this time that in desperation I decided that I must try to do something with my results. As you might imagine the MRC had a great library and a very helpful librarian, so I started to read journal articles and worked out how to analyse data and set it out. After a bit I began to correlate things and soon became quite engrossed in it. Patterns gradually emerged, and the library showed me how to relate results to other similar work. I started looking at what activities the subjects undertook and with the help of the literature I was able to assign an energy expenditure value to each and finally ended up with monthly patterns of energy expenditure. This did not mean a lot until I returned to the library and found papers on the energy expenditure of other and more readily understandable occupational groups – Fifeshire coal miners, Olympic athletes, Sandhurst cadets in training, office clerks, and schoolchildren. The energy expenditure of my subjects was apparently somewhere between Sandhurst cadets in training and carpenters. They spent an average of around 75 per cent of time between the sedentary activities of sitting, lying, and walking about inside, and this rose to 95 per cent of time during the dark months of winter. This sounds bad but it was not all that different from Sandhurst cadets in training, and the value for the sledge journey was 61 per cent of time in sedentary activities. We spent an average of 4 per cent of time in hard work outside. Once again it sounds bad, and this rose only to 14 per cent of time during the manhaul journey. On the other hand, Fife-shire miners only spent 11 per cent of time in hard work, and Sandhurst cadets 5 per cent. The conclusion was in line with that of Otto Edholm when he studied Sandhurst cadets that man is a much more sedentary animal than had previously been thought. One big and rather surprising finding was that my subjects spent only an average of 10 per cent of time out of doors during the year and in contact with the Antarctic climate. This all shows the pitfalls of making assumptions without scientific observations and measurements. There is a message there on wider issues.

My figures were beginning to make some sense, and I was getting quite excited about the whole thing. I had made sense of the activity pattern, and it was now time to do something with the climatic data. I had discovered all sorts of interesting things after rereading Dr Edholm's book. I did such correlations as creating double frequency tables of temperature and wind speed. I found that though we did get very low temperatures and very high wind speeds, these two things very rarely happened at the same time. When the temperature was very low, there was usually no wind velocity and as the wind velocity rose so did the temperature. All very interesting and important. I had to remember that my basic question was why was there no physiological change in response to life on a polar base when there were well-defined changes in response to heat. I had not quite realised it then but the beginning of an idea was forming in the recesses of my mind. Perhaps the men were not in contact with the Antarctic climate and thus with severe cold as much as we had thought, since they only spent an average of 10 per cent of their time out of doors. Also, if the temperature rose in sympathy with a rising wind velocity perhaps the cold stress was not as great as we had thought it could be from classical descriptive polar texts. Examining the time spent out of doors again I graphed this against the climatic data and found a precise correlation between monthly means of temperature and time spent out of doors. As the temperature fell the time out of doors also fell.

I felt that there was something there that I was missing and mulled it over in my mind for several days until one morning in the tube between Charing Cross and Hampstead I nearly had it. I could see something in the mist but it was not clear. I looked up from intense concentration and found I was at Belsize Park, so I got off and crossed over to take the tube back. I next came to as I was approaching Bank. I went back and forth and eventually alighted at Hampstead at twenty-five to eleven, but I felt I now had the answer. It seemed to me that there were three climatic states to be considered – the climate of the station, which I later called the met climate. Secondly, there was the climate to which the men were actually exposed and derived from my fifteen-minute measurements of climate as I followed the subjects around for twenty-four-hour periods. This I later called the exposure climate. Finally, there was the ultimate climate to which the body was exposed – namely the sub-clothing climate – as measured by Heinz Woolf's temperature-sensitive vest. This I later called the micro-climate. I could not get up Holly Hill fast enough to work on the detail of these climatic states. It transpired that the annual mean temperature of the met climate was –14.4 degrees Centigrade, but the monthly means varied with the seasons. The annual mean temperature of the exposure climate was +14.5 degrees Centigrade, and it did not vary with the seasons since people did not expose themselves to the low outside temperatures when it was very cold. This is a temperate climate. Finally, the annual mean temperature of the microclimate was 32.8 degrees Centigrade. This is a sub-tropical climate, which is reasonable since man has been shown to be basically a tropical animal.

During outside work or the manhaul sledge journey the micro-climate was a little lower and subject to mild variations since account needs to be taken of the highly efficient and variable layers of specialised clothing worn. It seems then that a reason why there was no physiological change in a man by virtue of his life on a polar base was because his body was not basically exposed to the cold. In other words this tropical animal had used his intelligence to modify the climate to which his body was fundamentally exposed by the use of clothing, heating, and housing. An Australian paper by Macpherson went a stage further and stated that since man is a tropical animal he has adapted to life in a temperate climate by changes which could be interpreted as evidence of acclimatisation to the cold but which we would call normal. When he returns to the tropics, he undergoes changes which we could call acclimatisation to heat but which are probably a return to his normal state. If this hypothesis is true, the changes found by virtue of life in a temperate climate are really the changes of cold acclimatisation, and it would be unrealistic to look for further changes of a physiological nature consequent on his life in a polar climate. Thus both human activity and true climatic exposure are very different from the pattern expected by casual observation.

Chapter 21

In Search of an MD

This was all quite fascinating to me, and I was now reading widely in the literature on environmental physiology. By the time the division returned from Aden, I was quite advanced with my own self-taught brand of analysis, and I had acquired a background of the relevant literature. This was just as well because when the members of the division returned from Aden no one really showed much interest in me – particularly the man who was supposed to be my supervisor! I think this was when my experience with the penguin project in the Antarctic first helped me because I had learned persistence. At about that point I looked into a drawer in my desk and found a book which turned out to be an MD thesis of the University of Cambridge and I read it. My conclusion was that if that is an MD then surely my work was worth an MD. I went to the library and looked at a few more theses and quietly decided to have a go myself. So after a lot of thought I started on the introduction and gradually enlarged the various sections.

I stopped going to the pictures – indeed going anywhere – and as soon as I got back to the mess I got out my old portable typewriter and typed away till the early hours. I did not mention it to anyone at this point. I was sharing a room at the MRC by this time with Henry Wyatt who had been in the Antarctic before me. When I came in one Monday morning, he said that he had been looking for some paper and had opened my desk drawer and found my introduction. He read it and said he thought it was very good and interesting. I told him of my aspirations and he fully supported them. Thus encouraged, I went to see my supervisor and said that I was considering writing an MD thesis and asked his opinion. "Positively not," he said. "We are not interested in theses here, only papers."

I was disappointed but, remembering the penguins, not defeated. With the brashness of youth I decided on the unusual step of circumventing my supervisor and made an appointment to see the all-high of the division, Dr Otto Gustavus Edholm. When I turned up, I was surprised to be shown right in. I was nearly shown right out again because I had only gained admission to the sanctum sanctorum because he thought I was a Dr Nixon who was apparently a big wig in the MRC. I said I just wanted to show him some of my results and would not take much time and before he could object I slapped one of my best graphs down on his desk. Fortunately, he quickly became interested and so I slapped down another and yet another until eventually I had had nearly an hour, and he was quite delighted. I then drew up all my reserves of courage and said I would dearly like to present this as an MD thesis, and I asked whether I could have his permission to approach Professor Garry at Glasgow. The answer was, "But my dear boy, you must, and tell him I sent you." After that hour, which I think was the turning point in my academic career, I had a splitting headache and a very fast pulse so I went straight across the road to the pub and had a large whisky.

Professor R. C. Garry was a great physiologist and a rather terrifying figure for students, so I approached him with some trepidation. He could, however, not have been nicer – he also became interested rapidly and when his secretary came in to say that the Dean wanted to talk to him urgently he replied, "Tell him I am busy talking to Dr Norman." That was a great feeling. When I eventually asked for his opinion on whether it was good enough and sufficient for an MD of Glasgow, he said, "But of course it is good enough for an MD – we only have to see what classification we can get."

Major Jim Adam was then living in the mess, and he gave me a lot of help with the scientific English and the precise and correct means of expression because at that time I had not even written a paper. There were several other men in the mess who were studying for higher degrees or writing papers. Alex Cummings had returned from the Argentine Island and was also writing up his results. Often about midnight the major would come round banging on the doors of these late workers, and we would all go off to an Indian restaurant in South Kensington called the Moti Mahal in the old Sunbeam Talbot that I had acquired with what was left of my Antarctic pay. The major presided over these midnight feasts. Having sent one of the waiters out for beer because the restaurant did not have a late licence, he demanded that the potatoes were removed from the mutton vindaloo because they gave him indigestion.

I used to catch the four-fifty from Paddington for Cheltenham and spend the weekend with Margaret and Jim. I acquired a thorough knowledge of the Cotswold villages because Jim was a very good host and delighted in showing off his very beautiful countryside. These were good days – living in the great Mess at Millbank during the week with weekends in Gloucester-shire. Once again my romantic Walter Mitty–like spirit had me involved in various imaginary adventures – the four-fifty from Paddington by Agatha Christie and the doings of the various dignitaries who travelled to London after a weekend in the country.

Preparing an MD is a big job and even my supervisor was becoming quite enthusiastic; the librarian loved looking for the most obscure references, the MRC photographer photographed my diagrams and showed me how to attach them to the pages, various people helped with the technical drawing of the diagrams (for there were no graphics packages in those days) – even Jim Gassor's cousin who was chief draughtsman at Doubty's factory in Cheltenham arranged for the more complex diagrams to be drawn and Jim Adam's secretary, Mrs Peck, did the typing. Typing was hair-raising because I needed six copies, and they had to be done with carbon paper and any mistakes meant that the whole page had to be typed again. Another problem was that Mrs Peck was in an advanced stage of pregnancy, and there was some doubt as to whether she would finish the thesis before she went into labour. She just made it. I had found a firm that bound theses and great was my feeling of joy and satisfaction when I finally saw it bound. I took it reverently to Sir Vivian Fuchs who, thinking that I was taking the piss out of Antarctic explorers and had read the report of our manhaul journey gave as his opinion, "Stuff and absolute bloody nonsense." This was fortunately before he had read it. Ten years later I went to a polar conference in Cambridge which he was opening, and he quoted it by the yard to my amazement and great pleasure.

The division of Human Physiology of the MRC was a fascinating place, and inevitably I got interested in other projects but mainly the artificial acclimatisation to heat project for the Army. The technique which they used was to exercise the soldiers in an environmental chamber set at 100 degrees Fahrenheit and 100 per cent humidity. They had to step up and down from a box at strict timing. They sweated profusely. Indeed the extent of acclimatisation was measured by the weight loss during a session which was determined by weighing them very accurately. Our job was to step up and down from the box to give the timing. It was hard work and we could lose 2 to 3 kilograms from sweating during a session. We repaired to the pub across the road to make up the fluid loss and the first pint of lager went straight down, the second a little slower, and the third at a normal speed but this resulted in a blinding headache. I therefore tried lemonade the next day and the result was a terrible feeling of weakness and lethargy. The third experiment was shandy, and this resulted in rapid recovery with no side effects. It is a form of fluid replacement which I have advocated widely after work in hot climates since then.

The next field trip was to Singapore, and I was invited to accompany the scientists. All I really had to do was stand at various parts of the jungle and measure pulse rates and temperatures as the soldiers were romped round a rigorous course. During the Aden course they had taken an ordinary bunch of soldiers, many of whom they suspected of just lying down when they were tired, so it was difficult to determine the effect of acclimatisation. On this occasion we took a regiment noted for its esprit de corps – a parachute regiment. The trouble was that they were so determined not to let the regiment down that when their temperatures went up to dangerous levels and they somewhat lost their marbles they refused to lie down on a stretcher and go to hospital – even defying their officers!

I thought Singapore was a marvellous place, and I developed a love affair with it that I still retain. Unfortunately I did not get back to

Singapore for several decades and though now greatly changed it has never lost its fascination for me. On that trip we stayed at the RAMC mess which was indeed a most beautiful site looking out to Sumatra. They had a curry luncheon every Sunday, and I think the whole of Singapore society came. There was a huge table stretching the length of the reception room, and it was laden four deep with different side dishes stretching the whole length of the reception room. This was the last of the British Raj, and it was great. I have tried to find that site on successive visits but I have not been able to find anyone who even remembers it. Discovering the Tanglin Club, however, provides considerable compensation. We also had a formal dinner in Raffles which at that time was lined in dark mahogany panelling. We had roast beef and Yorkshire pudding. On the way out I was amused to see that the cloakroom was filled with bowler hats and rolled umbrellas.

At last my MD was finished and my time with FIDS, the Army, and London was drawing to an end. Though I still saw myself as a surgeon I had developed a real interest in environmental physiology and medicine – indeed I had been invited to remain in the Army as an environmental physiologist by the director general, Sir Alexander Drummond to help with the work on heat. I was tempted because I liked London by this time, and I thought life in the mess was the last place where one could really live the life of a gentlemen. Otto Edholm next sent for me, and I wondered whether he was going to offer me a job also. He said that there had been an urgent request for a physiologist to help some investigators in Glasgow on some urgent work on carbon monoxide poisoning which was being carried out in Professor Charles Illingworth's department of surgery in Glasgow. He said the MRC were having difficulty in finding someone to send and would I be prepared to go since I came from Glasgow and was interested eventually in surgery. By that time I was practically drooling because Professor Illingworth was probably just about the most famous professor of surgery in the world at that time and his department a recognised breeding ground for surgeons of the future. I immediately agreed even though I knew nothing about carbon monoxide poisoning and very little about physiology, apart from the bit I had researched!

I had no complaints about National Service, however, because in addition to Northern Ireland, I had seen Montevideo, the Falkland Islands, South Georgia, the Antarctic, Tristan Da Cunha, Cape Town, Las Palmas, Istanbul, Bombay, Singapore, Ceylon, the Maldives and El Adam. In addition, I had completed and submitted my MD thesis before leaving National Service, and I was going to an appointment in the surgical Holy of Holies of the day as an MRC research fellow and, indeed, on the external staff of the Medical Research Council.

Who said, "Never volunteer for anything in the Army"? My adventure only happened because I grabbed the opportunity when Bill Sloman was looking for volunteers to go to the Falkland Islands Dependencies.

Acknowledgement.

I gratefully acknowledge the help and skill of Steven Hay, a medical photographer of Aberdeen University, who restored and edited the old images from half a century ago for this book.

About the Author

Nelson Norman was born in Paisley in 1932 and educated at Paisley Grammar School and Glasgow University. Fifty years ago he spent a year providing medical cover for a group of ten scientists at the Falkland Islands Dependencies Survey Base at Halley Bay, some eight hundred miles from the South Pole. During that time he gained first hand experience of the problems of healthcare of a remote community functioning in hazardous environmental conditions. He measured the cold exposure of the personnel and found that man – the tropical animal – used his intelligence to provide a more or less tropical micro climate for himself by the use of clothing, heating and housing. Although he was awarded the MD of Glasgow University for this work he proceeded to become an academic surgeon in the Universities of Glasgow and Aberdeen before establishing a second career in Remote Healthcare based upon the need to initiate a system of healthcare for the offshore oil industry in the North Sea and later in the Middle East. He founded the Institute of Environmental and Offshore Medicine at Aberdeen University in association with the late Dr Colin Jones of British Petroleum and subsequently the Centre for Offshore Health at the Robert Gordon University, Aberdeen before proceeding to a post in Community Medicine at the UAE University in the United Arab Emirates. He is an Emeritus Professor of Environmental Medicine at Aberdeen University and an Adjunct Professor of Community Medicine at the UAE University in Abu Dhabi and has been a visiting Professor of Surgery at the University of Kinshasa in Zaire and a visiting Professor of Community Medicine at Memorial University, St John's, Newfoundland. He is now President of the Institute of Remote Healthcare.

Lightning Source UK Ltd.
Milton Keynes UK
14 November 2009

146202UK00002BA/35/P